For
Monsignor. K
June — 1964

Love
is forever

and so, what else can
one do —

87

Henri Daniel-Rops
Michel Riquet
Gustave Thibon
Jacques Madaule
Mary Pyle: translator

Scepter Books

First published 1964

PRINTED IN THE REPUBLIC OF IRELAND

Library of Congress Catalog Card Number 64-20887.

This translation from *Le Couple Chrétien* (Le Livre
Contemporain, Paris), was printed by Dublin Univer-
sity Press Ltd for Scepter Publishers Ltd, 144 Lower
Baggot Street, Dublin 2 and Scepter Publishers,
30 North La Salle Street, Chicago 2. Nihil obstat:
Finnianus Cronin, o.f.m., Censor Theol. deput.
Imprimi potest: ✝ Joannes Carolus, Archiep.
Dublinen., Hiberniae Primas, Dublin, die 11 feb-
ruarii, anno 1964.

Contents

Foreword

At first glance it may seem like beating a dead horse to bring out a book of essays on the indissolubility of marriage at this late date. My first reaction was, ' Whatever for? ' — and I suspect yours may be too.

Surely no one who has witnessed the decline of the family, the accumulation of fractured lives and hopes and homes, would be stubborn enough to hail divorce as a milestone of human progress. And no one is mounting a soapbox any more to demand that the Church get in step with the times on this question. So what is the point in resurrecting it? Well, I must say I learned by reading on, as I hope you will too.

I can now tell you that it is of vast importance to consider *why* divorce has failed to help either people or marriage and *why* the Church had to be uncompromising, unequivocal, and seemingly unsympathetic on this question — even long before the results of wholesale divorce were strewn for all eyes to see.

In that *why* (which these essays place squarely in the nature of the family) lies the answer to another related problem currently plaguing mankind — the question of family limitation. For, as the theologians show, it is exactly in the fruitfulness of marriage that one finds the key to understanding its stability and permanence.

Gustave Thibon, in an essay as complete as it is balanced, develops the reasons for the ' always ' of marriage — reasons implicit in the nature of the family and in the sacramental character of marriage.

Is the Church the enemy of love when she insists on the permanence of the marriage bond? On the contrary, 'by imposing on love the obligation not to die', she 'puts time at the service of love', and offers a purifying process for all the crises and illnesses of love's growing, he tells us.

How one young couple with a bone-deep regard for the *institution* of marriage turned a castle full of such crises into the means of sanctification is the subject of Daniel Rops' sketch of Louis IX and his wife Marguerite.

But what of the suffering in marriages where there is apparently no such deep conviction about the institution, where there is, moreover, no love? What about the unhappiness of the individuals involved, the 'revolt of subjective inclinations against a universal law which protects the happiness of others', but which seems to condemn *them* to a bitter and barren future? Thibon's reply (stated in a somewhat different idiom in Jacques Madaule's essay) is, 'What of the soldier who is asked by his country to die in order to save the national well-being in which he will not share? . . . Is it the law which is too hard for man or is it that man is too soft for the law?' — that law, we had better all remember, which must itself be protected 'against the thousand vicissitudes of instinct and self-interest.' And he reminds the sufferer to make Christian use of his suffering so that 'what miscarries in time can blossom in eternity.'

If I had to choose a favorite from the many luminous thoughts Thibon presents in his short essay, it would be this :

'Today . . . we find growing up a kind of mystique about marriage which is preoccupied more with the quality of the personal link between husband and wife than with its social preservation. The tendency is to see the essence of marriage more and more in acts of love . . . by which two beings join and mingle their destinies. The rest — fidelity to each other, procreation and upbringing of children, the welfare of society, etc. — flows from this source as the temporal flows from the eternal. This is the myth of " companions for eternity." '

Here, it seems to me, he has identified a mysterious malady from which too many marriages, and too much writing on marriage is suffering in ' this period of morbid hyperesthesia of self and crass insistence on personal rights.'

One has only to pick up some of the current literature to find confirmation not only that the love relationship is everything but that ' the happiness of the individual is thought of as an *unconditional* right,' and any contradiction of it a ' matter for indignation and scandal.' For instance :

> ' Socio-psychological research can show us that married people of today consider the problems of marriage fundamentally in terms of conjugal love, and they consider the Natural Law arguments, neglecting the reality of married love and relegating it to a secondary and non-essential place, as unrealistic and even immoral.'

or, > ' . . . the use of sex as an expression of love should be recognized as an end in itself, with a validity in itself, apart from its potential generative uses.'

or, > ' This reviewer wishes that Father — had not been hampered, as so many Catholic writers

> have been, by the traditional terminology about the purposes of marriage. Surely the central reason-for-being of marriage, both as an institution and as a sacrament, cannot be other than the partnering and companioning of man and woman for the sanctifying of each other and of the children if any.'

One is forced to conclude either that the Author of marriage didn't have enough twentieth-century expertise to put marriage together right in the first place, or else that the Church, to whom he entrusted the guardianship of human love, simply doesn't know the players, let alone the score and the object of the game. So it has plainly become our mission to straighten out God and/or the Church and make them respectable again.

Some months ago, having wearied of the word-explosion on this subject, I prepared a dissenting article which appeared nationally under the title, ' Love, O Love, O Careful Love.' The response, which turned out to be both a surprise and a delight, confirmed my own observations about the working-together of the ends of marriage and gave existential proof of the firm teaching that the function of mutual love ' is to bind parents together for the purpose of creating an optimum atmosphere for the best raising of their young.'

This same thought is developed in Father Riquet's essay : ' It could be said that the objective of marriage is to grow and perfect human nature by the union of man and woman in the family which they found, increase, and govern in the interests of the good of all its members. And in the specific case of Christians who acquire the sacramental grace of matrimony, it can be said that its objective is to grow and to perfect the Mystical Body of Christ by the union of man and woman in the family which they found, increase, and govern in the interests of the spiritual well-being of each of its members.

The special value of this book lies in its careful attention to the nature of marriage at a time when this concept seems to have fallen on evil days.

At present, it is not the permanence of marriage which is under direct attack but the fruitfulness of marriage. Yet so perfectly interwoven are these two principles in the fabric of family that neither one can be extricated without ruining the goods. It is always Christian marriage itself which suffers, no matter which of its aspects is under fire in any given era. What Thibon says about the principle of indissolubility applies just as well to the principle of fruitfulness, and it would be a good thing to start applying it that way : 'The principle of indissoluble marriage is like a gate attacked by the tempest of passions and personal interests; if it is half opened it is no longer possible to keep it on its hinges, and the hurricane will engulf everything.'

Anyone who is concerned with marriage education (all of us, I hope) would be better for listening to this preceptive man's frequent reminder that whatever it has pleased God to join together, man has not the right to put asunder. For my part, I take this to include not only man and wife, but the primary and secondary ends of marriage, the blessings of marriage, and the marital act and procreation — not failing to reflect, with Father Riquet, that 'only a love which finds its principle and its end in God will succeed in safe-guarding the hierarchy of the main objectives of marriage . . . the freedom of a love which rejoins the divine love.'

JANE HANOVER ADAMS

Portrait of a Christian Couple

Henri Daniel-Rops

'In this ring, all my love.'

On 27th May 1234, in the Cathedral of Sens, the young king Louis IX was married to Marguerite of Provence. He was barely twenty years old, and she was just over fourteen: two children. The marriage had been arranged to the advantage of the French crown, by Blanche of Castile, widow of the late king and regent of the kingdom, a most formidable woman, according to all accounts. Love played no part in the match.

It was a good political match which, with an eye to a future union of lands, joined to the Capetian throne this lovely southern county, already French by so many human ties, but still officially part of the Holy Roman Empire. The idea probably took shape in the shrewd mind of Queen Blanche and her advisors. The Count of Provence, Beranger le Grand, nicknamed the Mistral, had looked favourably on the great interest of the government of Paris in his eldest daughter. When Giles de Flagy, the French ambassador, appeared before him on a flimsy pretext, his mouth full of honeyed words, Beranger was not deceived as to his real purpose. The matter was duly arranged.

The two people most concerned had probably not been consulted at all. The notion that her son might have personal views on the matter would certainly not have troubled the Regent, who was accustomed to seeing him carry out her wishes in everything. And as for the little princess, how at her age could she have understood the wedding as being anything other than a very gay celebration, after which, overwhelmed with presents, she would leave on the arm of a handsome cavalier. Three days before the ceremony they had not yet seen each other; all he knew of her was what had been reported by the ambassador responsible for the negotiations, and she knew no more of the amorous qualities of her husband than she could learn during the journey from Mgr Cornu, Archbishop of Sens, and her own uncle, William, Bishop of Valence, who had come to fetch her. That was probably not very much.

According to our modern ideas about marriage, this union between the future Saint Louis and Marguerite would seem to have taken place under the least favourable auspices. No physical attraction to each other or affinity of mind had anything to do with it. The worst bourgeois marriage of convenience, arranged to augment income and investments, rarely is so lacking to the point of disdaining what seems to us indispensable in a marriage — understanding, harmony, feeling for each other, in a word, love.

Worse still: this young couple broached the uncertainties and hazards of married life with a severe handicap: nothing less than the constant presence of the least discreet of mothers-in-law. It is common knowledge that Blanche of Castile was a woman of the highest virtue, a perfect mother, a queen in the fullest sense of the word, and the historians of Saint Louis were right in saying that the most admirable of all the kings of France owed much of what he was to his mother. It is no less true that this domineering Spaniard, accustomed to treating her son as a little boy (with all the appearances of ceremonial deference, of course), used to intervening in all his actions, and even to directing his interior life, did not change her attitude towards him when he was married. For many long years Marguerite was faced with Blanche's constant influence from which her husband, although now adult, refused to escape. This was a considerable addition to the difficulties inherent in marriage, and today we might well expect such a union to be unsuccessful. That it was no such thing, that on the contrary Louis and Marguerite can even be held up as an exemplary couple, is a striking demonstration of the intrinsic strength which is contained in the Christian sacrament of marriage, when it is taken seriously.

Love, which had not been invited to the ceremony, overtook the young couple quickly. Louis and Marguerite had not yet made their triumphal entry into

Paris when they saw each other in the radiant light
of youthful passion. For both of them love was an
unknown land, which they were each exploring for
the first time. The little princess from Provence,
brought up in the courtly atmosphere of Aix, Arles
and Avignon, was certainly no more ingenuous and
unsophisticated than this tall, reserved young man,
whose chaste mother had brought him up in the most
absolute purity. Neither arrived at the altar with the
worn out emotions and dulled senses of so many
young couples. But could not even this joy of mutual
discovery have been an illusion?

Their love, of course, was not purely physical. We
know, from a reliable source, that Louis entered into
the state of marriage with that simple, truly Christian
gravity with which, all his life, he approached even
the simplest of his actions. The proceedings for his
canonisation, which contained many frank statements
and, above all, the witness of queen Marguerite's
confessor, tells us that before consummating the marriage, after the benediction the young king spent three
whole nights in prayer and that he did not enter the
bridal chamber until the fourth day. (Even then he
was not to spend the whole night there because Blanche
was keeping a close watch, and as soon as she considered that her son had been there long enough to
fulfil his duties as a husband, she sent for him and
ordered him back to his own apartment.) This refined
use of the sacrament will no doubt appear exaggerated
to many young couples today: but it was to this that

the marriage of Louis and Marguerite owed its solidity when the flame of passion began to die down.

There is no doubt but that in the early days of their marriage these two young people were truly in love. If they were both inexperienced and innocent, both displayed a great propensity for love; as Saint Augustine said, they ' loved to love.' Louis was a magnificent youth, with a fine build, fair and fresh in complexion, with pale blue eyes; he was manly without being excessively heavy or strong, energetic and well-balanced, and possessed both charm and intelligence, a serious sweetness and a grave serenity of a kind which make women feel that in such a man they could find security. Smaller than he, slim and highly-strung, with dark hair and sparkling black eyes, Marguerite seems to have been more piquante than really pretty, charm and gaiety making up for the lack of perfection in her features. A boy of twenty and a girl of fifteen did not need much more to find each other attractive.

Joinville, a good source, bears witness to this youthful passion. At Pontoise castle, where the pair liked best to live, their bedrooms were exactly one above the other, for it was not considered proper for them to share a room, or even to have adjoining rooms. But a fortunate inspiration of the architect had resulted in a spiral staircase between the rooms, which made things considerably easier. Their love was ardent for about two years and was not cooled either by the queen's pregnancies, or the queen mother's exasperating interference.

For, Joinville also notes, ' the severity of Queen Blanche towards her little daughter-in-law was constant. One manifestation of this was her irritating habit of entering the apartments of one or other at the least opportune moments, so tactlessly that the good gentlemen-ushers on duty outside the royal chambers, who were sorry for the lovers, would knock on the door with their staves so that Louis could hastily regain his bed and so avoid the remonstrances of his mother.' And at the birth of their first child, while Louis, greatly moved, was beside the bed of his wife, his formidable mother took him by the hand to lead him away, exclaiming that this was not his place, and only left him in peace because his young wife protested half-fainting and in tears. Everything contributed to make this love strong and passionate, even the obstacles. However, was it this which was to sustain the married life of Louis and Marguerite? Inside the wedding ring the young husband had had inscribed ' In this ring all my love.' But the phrase admits of several different meanings. This love : was it to endure throughout life; or did the expression merely mean a promise of absolute fidelity?

It seems to have been the second interpretation which won. In marriage there are times when circumstances and psychological evolution make a crisis almost final. The first takes place some eighteen months or two years after the wedding, when the flame of mutual discovery has cooled a little, and when the young couple have got over the thrill of bringing into the world a child born from their love. It is at this stage that the realities of life become prominent and constraining and the question arises of whether the couple will be able to present a united front. For in the final analysis what matters is not that these crises appear, but the way in which couples meet them and react to them. (And this also holds good for those crises which come in maturity and threaten men and women between the ages of forty and fifty.)

There is no reason to think that between Louis and Marguerite there was any real crisis, but there are many indications that the passionate love of their youth did not last throughout their entire lives. Indeed Joinville is explicit on this fact. ' I have spent five years in the company of the king ', he writes, ' during which time he never spoke of the queen or of his children, either to me or to anyone else, and it seems to me that it was not just his manner, but that he was in fact estranged from his wife and children.' It could be argued that here is a modest and very natural reserve, a pleasant change from the usual indiscretions, but when a man bears in his heart a really great love, can he at this point keep silent, even in the company of his best friend? It seems certain that as this love developed it became less exacting, less imperious, certainly without dying altogether, but without monopolising the best part of their lives.

To tell the truth they were extremely dissimilar and their personalities were not exactly formed to sympathise with each other. Louis was never shaken from his calmness, his restraint, his evenness of temper, nor from his inexorable requirement of moral perfection in everything. He was never seen to be angry, he never spoke a light or a vain word. Marguerite, who became more and more impulsive and exuberant as she grew older, showed the noisy gaiety and the love for amusement and clothes of a pretty woman from the South. The king was too good a Christian to bear his wife any malice because of this difference. But we can imagine, without offending his memory, that he might have been exasperated by it from time to time.

On the other hand, when the first fires of passion are dying down, husband and wife can find themselves perfectly united through mutual interests and a shared life together; but it was soon obvious that for several reasons Marguerite hardly ever shared her husband's interests. Firstly, because Queen Blanche involved herself much in the king's life and did not allow Marguerite to take part in it; and continued all her life to act as adviser to her son. Also, whereas the mother of Saint Louis approached politics with reflection, astuteness and determination, his young wife allowed her personal feelings to run away with her. Because she was jealous of her sister Eleanor, wife of Henry III of England, and hated Charles of Anjou, Louis' brother, who had married her own sister Beatrice, she did not hesitate to upset royal diplomacy by intriguing against them in Rome and in Spain. Very soon, Louis felt he could confide nothing of importance to this headstrong creature, and his distrust was strikingly illustrated when, on his departure for the second crusade, he gave the administration of the kingdom not to Marguerite, but to two members of the royal council. Thus, it was not on the basis 'the job of kingsmanship' that the two could have founded their love.

It is hardly necessary to add that neither was it through love for their children that Louis and Marguerite could have rediscovered the passion of their youth. They had many children — six sons and five daughters : rather too many, perhaps, for the event of a birth to count greatly in their intimate lives; it is well enough known that in large families where the mother is overwhelmed with chores and worries and the father has to show infinite patience, the deep union of the parents is maintained only by a healthy love and at the cost of constant effort. Louis and Marguerite should have shared their hopes and sorrows — and their greatest sorrow was the death at the age of sixteen of their eldest son, Louis, who showed signs of taking after his father — but we gather from Joinville that his family did not hold first place in the heart of the king.

This then is the framework within which the conjugal relations of Louis and Marguerite developed. Did their marriage surmount the crises? One suspects that it did from various details recorded by the chronicler. Some of them are amusing : one day when Marguerite was remonstrating with her husband for dressing too soberly for his high position, he replied that he felt a similar displeasure to see her so concerned with clothes, jewels and fripperies, and that he would change his manner of dress when she changed hers; upon which the queen quickly dropped the subject. . . Others are more serious: at a time when Louis' health was giving cause for concern, Marguerite, foreseeing a regency, hit on the plan of extracting from the crown prince Philip a secret promise to obey her in everything until the age of thirty. When St Louis learnt of it he was, as we can imagine, greatly saddened, and his confidence in his wife was reduced.

Hence, the relationship between Louis and Marguerite can in no way be painted in the conventional colours of an unchanging and unmixed happiness. That is not to say that their marriage was unhappy; in marriage, even more than in anything else, happiness is largely a matter of will-power. One is happy when one wishes to be, and this is why nothing is more pernicious than a certain taste for melancholy, a kind of admission of failure, which makes so many marriages come to grief. In human terms, the married love of Louis and Marguerite does not appear to have been particularly exalted; but this did not render their love any less real, solid and unshakeable. For it was love in a Christian sense.

It is known, through the investigation conducted before his canonisation, to what extent faith was associated with the love Louis bore to Marguerite. After the brief period where youthful passion spoke loudly

in his heart (and we have seen moreover that he could
keep it in check) there is no doubt but that the saintly
king loved his wife in God, through Christ and for
him. He did not separate his marriage from his desire
to lead a holy life. William of Saint-Pathuq, the
queen's confessor, records that Saint Louis imposed
complete chastity on his wife at certain times of the
year, Advent and Lent, Friday and Saturday of every
week, the eves of festivals, and the festivals themselves
after communion. These details, indiscreetly provided
by the historian, will make many Christians smile
today; in this discipline, to which Marguerite con-
sented, are we not obliged to see the proof of a very
noble wish, that of giving even to carnal pleasure its
spiritual quality? In this, it is certain that Marguerite
shared in the very saintliness of her husband.

To this union, founded on the law of Christ,
each brought that honest willingness which, when
passionate love has been quenched, is the best way
to a more durable love. It is hardly necessary to say
that the fidelity of the king was complete and absolute.
Joinville records, however, that with his wife he was
never seen to be other than courteous and reserved,
that he was never caught unawares on terms of
familiarity with any woman other than his wife.
From this point of view, the motto on the wedding
ring held true all his life: ' In this ring, all my love '
for he had no other love than that which was blessed
at Sens.

It goes without saying that he expected his wife
to observe the same principle, and the records tell us

that he supervised Marguerite's entourage closely, and would dismiss any woman to whom was attached the slightest scandal. But wise as were these precautions, they do not seem to have been in the least justified by the conduct of the queen. All that we know of her shows her to have been entirely faithful, truly loving her husband, admiring him and accepting second place in his life, the first belonging to God. She was certainly a blameless wife : that she was not more, that she sometimes even crossed or exasperated her husband, is human nature, and Marguerite was not a saint.

All the same, there were moments in their married life when their love was raised high above what is normal, and when, exalted by the heroism of true Christians, it reached the sublime. One of these occasions arose at the time of the first crusade, on which, although pregnant, Marguerite had insisted on accompanying her husband : when he was taken prisoner, the queen, confined in Damiette, took the situation in hand, encouraged the men, worked to pay her husband's ransom and from her bed asserted herself like a true leader — indeed, a worthy wife of him who, by his calm courage, had won the respect of the Arabs. One day, when all seemed lost, she compelled her old equerry to swear to kill her if the Moslems were about to take her. A Christian queen must not fall into the hands of the infidels. By such acts one recognises the believer and the wife of a saint.

On yet another occasion, the witness she gave was, in a sense, more Christian than that of her husband himself. Haunted by the desire to renounce power, to consecrate himself entirely to God, doubtless in the ranks of the monks of Saint Francis, Louis came to ask his wife's permission to do so. It was she who showed him his true duty, and told him that it was more difficult and more meritorious to serve the Lord where he had placed him, in the midst of overwhelming responsibilities and cares, than to relinquish the burden by taking refuge in the holy destitution of the poor man of Assisi. By keeping her husband on the throne, by forcing him to look his real destiny in the face, this woman, perhaps a little frivolous, a little too impulsive, a little too meddlesome, managed to understand the real depth of Christian duty: what a touch of light it throws on her portrait!

Such was the marriage of Saint Louis and Marguerite of Provence. Perhaps some would prefer to see them ideally united in total harmony, rising together heavenwards at the end of a road without thorns. Other human couples have known this experience in which human love is, as it were, devoured by the divine flame and is entirely spiritualised by it. It was not so for this most saintly king and his wife; and it is in this that their example seems to us to be so full of significance. The saintliness of the husband did not prevent him from finding difficulties and stumbling-blocks on his domestic path, but it did serve to make these difficulties and stumbling-blocks turn to the mutual sanctification of his wife and himself. That is why Saint Francis de Sales, the Christian thinker who has spoken best about marriage, its hazards and its demands, very properly chose as the most perfect example of a Christian couple Saint Louis and Marguerite.

For, the Christian sacrament of marriage does not prevent the union of man and woman from being difficult, problematic and hazardous, but it is a fact that the difficulties and the dangers help to perfect and sanctify the two souls which unite with each other.

Motives for Marriage

Michel Riquet

Why does one marry? Why should one marry? The two questions are not identical. The first only calls for a description of the usual behaviour of human beings, a report on the usual motives of those who marry. The second, on the other hand, suggests a moral, and even a metaphysical and theological intention. It is no longer a question of what men and women think of and are preoccupied with when they envisage marriage, but what objectives they should aim at to respect the order and hierarchy of its aims, so as not to risk finding themselves in conflict with the demands of nature and the designs of Providence.

Obviously this way of talking and of approaching the problem has meaning only for those who believe in Providence and believe that everything has a nature and purpose. This is not true of certain forms of existentialism, nor of communism.

However, one can try to satisfy one and the other by beginning with an analysis of facts, behaviour and tendencies, to discover in these the profound demands of nature which indicate the intentions of Providence.

In all these nations whose history can be reconstructed by historical research, marriage usually appears as a social institution, controlled and protected by the laws of the city or of the tribe and consecrated by religion.

The most ancient of the known moral codes, such as, for example, those of the Egyptians and the Babylonians, the Hindus and the Chinese, contain explicit instructions about the status and mutual rights and duties of persons united through marriage : husband and wife, parents and children. One and all show a common preoccupation : to ensure the stability, continuity and the development of the family, the basic cell of cities and peoples. By and large, it is true to say that the western world remains attached to this outlook in theory, although actual practice may deviate from it considerably. In the abstract, to marry is to settle down, start a home and become domesticated, and these expressions all reveal the same desire for stability in a shared life and an association which one hopes will give both man and wife advantages, security and a future which they could not hope for while living alone and independent of each other. This security which the individuals seek in marriage is also what governments wish and hope for. As the jurist, Jean Bodin, says : 'It is possible that the Republic would be worth nothing, if the families which are its pillars have unsound foundations.'

The attention accorded to this civic aspect of marriage leads one to consider it as a legal contract which is protected in the interests of public order. From this fact it has frequently resulted that social, economic and political motives had a great, and too often exclusive, influence on a large number of marriages: this is certainly true of the nineteenth century and it is not unknown today. It is well known under what circumstances the marriages of princes formerly took place. But what landowner, lawyer or businessman of today does not also plan to make the marriage of his son or daughter enhance his own prestige? A son-in-law is chosen who is capable of developing his wife's inheritance. The young law student will choose a great lawyer as a father-in-law, mixing, as they say, ' business with pleasure.' Indeed, a whole middle class has been established, developed and enlarged by a policy of matrimonial alliances modelled on those of feudal lords and princes.

Not only are parents at fault. Their children are often quite prepared to act in this way themselves. What about all those medical students who married into a practice, or those younger sons who looked for a young lady with private means? This fusion of the marriage ties with inheritances and legacies has assured the prosperity of many families, but also the unhappiness, public or private, of many others.

Confronted with this ' social ' attitude to marriage, there is all the more reason to define and defend the rights of love. The heart has its reasons which the law has no need to know: in the Christian

Middle Ages the subtle conventions of courtly love, the romance of Tristan and Isolde, constantly emphasised, with apparent respect for the laws of marriage, the rights of the heart and of passion. Since one could not marry for love, one loved outside marriage. But in order to safeguard the promises of fidelity which husband and wife officially exchanged before God and man, the following principle was imposed and more or less strictly observed: 'He is incapable of giving anything at all [in courtly love] who demands the entire possession of his mistress. What becomes reality is no longer love.' [1]

With less elegance Karl Marx and Frederick Engels wrote in 1848, in the first Manifesto of the Communist Party: 'Our bourgeoisie, not content with having the wives and daughters of their proletarians at their disposal, not to speak of common prostitutes, take the greatest pleasure in seducing each other's wives. Bourgeois marriage is in reality a system of wives in common.'

The middle-class novelists of the nineteenth and twentieth centuries, from Balzac to Proust, from Gide to Mauriac, have given grounds for this judgment by their description of the behaviour of their world. They did not invent, lie or even exaggerate and what they describe still happens today. However, it is not true to suggest that this kind of marriage is unique to the upper classes or the middle class. It is also found in other sectors of society; and although paternal ambition and plans may less often stand in the way of passion and feeling, it still happens that the average man seeks in marriage advantages, guarantees and security for the future without consenting to impose rigorously on himself the fidelity which he hopes, expects and demands.

No matter what his social background, man finds the same deep tendencies towards selfishness and love, towards the pleasure found in carnal passion and the heroism which goes beyond itself in renunciation and sacrifice. One and all experience at puberty the same impulses of the sexual instinct, the same confused desire both to give and to possess, to find a stable equilibrium of these contradictory tendencies which lead us to conquer, dominate, possess, and at the same time to submit to another free person. One can look on marriage as an exchange or contract, thanks to which one is certain of receiving as much as one gives, *do ut des,* giving, giving (however, since each values more highly what he gives than what he receives, each finally declares himself to be the loser). Or else, one can assume that marriage consists simply of some limited mutual services, and so one looks to free love as a means of satisfying one's desires. We know to what undisciplined behaviour these incoherent solutions lead.

What then, in view of all this, is the Christian solution?

We have all heard this complaint from someone who is tired of being a Christian : ' Christianity is not fair to the flesh, it suppresses it.' But, of course, the Church has never ratified or justified this statement. Saint Paul himself warned his disciple Timothy against these ' pretensions of imposters . . . who bid them abstain from marriage, and from certain kinds of food, although God has made these for the grateful enjoyment of those whom faith has enabled to recognise the truth '. And he concludes : 'All is good that God has made, nothing is to be rejected : only we must be thankful to him when we partake of it, then it is hallowed for our use by God's blessing and the prayer which brings it.' [2]

Against the Manicheans of all kinds, the Montanists and the Albigenses, the Councils from the fifth to the sixteenth century repeat the profession of faith of Florence : ' Since God has so willed, he has, in his goodness, made all creatures, as much spiritual as physical, good, certainly, since created by him who is supremely good, but changing because made of nothing. All nature as nature is good.' So, woe to him who condemns human marriage, and regards the procreation of children with horror; woe to him who pretends that the creation of all flesh is not the work of God but of evil spirits; woe to whomever condemns bodily nourishment as impure. ' Not only the virgins and the continent, but also married people who are pleasing to God, have a true faith and a good life and deserve to attain to everlasting life.'

Christianity takes into account the whole reality of man. The real man is a thing of soul and body. It is significant that man is born, is nourished, grows and develops like all mammals and, like them, having reached puberty he feels within himself, avid and demanding, the voice of the species which wants, through him, to reproduce itself, and to this end pushes him to join himself to a being similar to him but of a different sex.

The Bible makes no mystery of it. And Jesus did not hesitate to repeat to the crowd the realistic words of Genesis:

> ' God created man in his own image,
> To the image of God created he him
> Male and female created he them.'

And he said: 'A man, therefore, will leave his father and mother and will cling to his wife, and the two will become one flesh; what God, then, has joined, let not man put asunder.' [3]

One cannot say more clearly that God wanted sexuality with all that it comprises, including this intimate union between man and woman, essential to marriage. After telling how God created man ' male and female ' and said to him ' increase and multiply ', Genesis concludes: ' God saw all things that he had made, and they were very good.'

What right then could a Christian have to malign the sexes and their necessary relations?

However, if he reads further in the Book of Genesis he will soon find that even the best things are capable of being abused. The flood came to curb the corruption of public morals, in which sexual licentiousness, under divers forms, does not seem to have been the least cause: ' All flesh had corrupted its way.'

The ruin of Sodom and Gomorrah penalises a perversion of sexuality which Saint Paul was to denounce as an especially infamous depravity of the pagan world, from which came many other vices.

Man is thus capable of perverting, by an irregular or unnatural usage, what in itself is healthy and beneficial. This applies also to sexuality and it is necessary therefore to know the meaning and the purpose of marriage to be able to judge its morality. With his logical vigour Saint Thomas Aquinas wrote:

' Wherefore it is no sin if one, by the dictate of reason, makes use of certain things in a fitting manner and order for the end to which they are adapted, provided this end be something truly good. Now just as the preservation of bodily nature of one individual is a true good, so, too, is the preservation of the nature of the whole species a very great good. And just as the use of food is directed to the preservation of life in the individual, so is the use of venereal acts directed to the preservation of the whole human race. Wherefore just as the use of food can be without sin, if it be taken in due manner and order, as required for the welfare of the body, so also the use of venereal acts can be without sin, provided they be performed in due manner and order, in keeping with the end of human procreation.' [4]

And:

' The purpose of the sexual organs is the procreation and education of children; and therefore any use of these organs which is not directed towards the generation and proper education of children is in itself disordered. But it is clear that any use of these organs outside the union of man and woman is not ordained to the procreation of children. Neither is any union of man and woman outside the law of matrimony ordained to the education due to the children : for the law of matrimony is instituted to exclude such free access which makes it difficult to establish the parenthood . . . and therefore the concern of the father for the education of the children easily disappears : and this would go contrary to the needs of nature.' [5]

This view is undeniably correct. It justifies the constant attitude of the Church, her doctrine and her discipline, which from the beginning right up to the last Encyclical *Casti Connubii* forbids everything which tends to mutilate nature by deflecting the sexual act from its fertile destination by practices, artificial means, or abuses which degrade, pervert and corrupt those men and women who give in to them.

However, we may ask ourselves if the procreation and upbringing of children must be considered as the sole purpose, the only end and one essential of marriage, as of marital relations.

The Creator certainly said to the man and woman whom he had just created : ' Increase and multiply.' But in a second account, complementary to the first, God is heard to say : ' It is not good for man to be alone, let us make him a help like unto himself.' And when Adam cries in the presence of Eve ' This now is bone of my bones, and flesh of my flesh ', the Bible adds : 'A man shall cleave to his wife : and they shall be two in one flesh.' [6]

The intimacy of man and woman appears here independent of the procreation of children, as a benefit and a necessity. It is not good for man to be alone; but it insists that man does not escape from his solitude except by the fertility of marriage, the only origin of peoples and societies.

The Code of Canon Law promulgated by Pope Benedict in 1917, which condenses the jurisprudence and the legislation of the Church, declares that : ' The primary end of marriage is the procreation and education of children; the secondary end is mutual help and the cure for concupiscence. Its essential characteristics are unity and indissolubility which, in a Christian marriage, find a particular strength by reason of the Sacrament ' (Canon 1013).

There are thus two objectives; procreation and up-bringing of children on the one hand, mutual help and the appeasement of concupiscence on the other. But one is stated to be primary and the other secon-dary. However, the Code specifies that ' sterility does not prevent marriage nor render it invalid ' (Canon 1068). And theologians are unanimous in explaining that sterility does not prevent a married couple from attaining the secondary end of marriage : mutual help and the appeasement of concupiscence. ' Secondary ' does not have here the sense of accessory or optional, as is shown by the fact that the inability of one of the partners to accomplish the marriage act, hence to assuage concupiscence, constitutes an impediment and causes the nullity of the contracted marriage. It may be deduced from this that the secondary end is itself also essential in marriage; that it is sufficient to justify it and to make it desirable when circumstances such as physiological or pathological sterility do not permit the attainment of the primary end.

Biologically, sexuality exists only for the increasing of the animal or vegetable species; it is ordained for the purpose of reproduction. But without departing from the biological point of view, it is equally true that through the exercise of the sexual function individuals find a blossoming of their being which perfects them harmoniously.

Before the child is born, and even if it cannot be born, the man and woman who join together and become one single flesh in a complete communion of life build an experience, realise a gift of the self to the other-than-self, in an interpenetration of their physical and spiritual being, specifically relating and pertaining to the conjugal act. Here they should find a fulfilment which it is legitimate and perfectly honest and desirable for them to seek as long as it does not exclude, by positive artifice, the normal fruit of their union, the child.

It is the prerogative of each person not to allow himself to be an instrument or a means subordinated to the good of some creature. A being endowed with intelligence and liberty can only subordinate himself to the supreme Good, to God. He could never, without renouncing what constitutes his greatness, sub-ordinate himself or sacrifice himself to the animal species of which he is the most superior specimen.

In marriage, and in the conjugal act itself, husband and wife will rightly see their mutual perfecting. The child is normally included as sharing in this, not certainly as a means, for he too has rights as an individual, but as a member of the family community, with the conjugal experience in which his parents seek fulfilment through each other and with each other, as he himself with them and by them will proceed from an embryonic life to the fulness and physical and spiritual maturity of the perfected man.

Only a love which finds its principle and its end in God will succeed in safeguarding the hierarchy of the main objectives of marriage. It alone excludes and prevents enslavement of one to the caprice of the other. If the couple meet sexually, it will only be in a healthy and normal fecundity, with the joint wish not to become engulfed by sex, but on the contrary to find in it the upward path which will lead them to discover over and above love on the human plane the joys and the freedom of a love which rejoins the divine love.

When seized by a powerful sensual attraction, man emerges from his previous limited desire for individual preservation. He begins to be interested, and how intensely, in someone other than himeslf, someone who seems to be a divine complement to himself. In their mutual attraction each discovers and completes the other. Love of self here finds its place, but in terms of opening to the love of another-than-self. For, this other, which can only be attached to oneself by attaching oneself to him, appears at the same time both similar and different, not just a replica, a mere double of oneself, but a complementary being.

It is complementary in its sex, first of all; for the science of physiology teaches us that there is not a particle of our body which does not bear the imprint of masculinity or femininity. Even the skeletons of man and woman differ, and also the muscles and the hormones.

Nature builds one for battle, racing, hunting : the constructive and creative activities. It prepares the other for maternity, for the tasks of rearing children : from the duties of feeding and developing the health and vigour of the body, to those which shape the character, and make the soul receptive and sensitive. Indispensable to each other in engendering and bringing up the child, man and woman complete each other by their different qualities in all the forms of activity and creation. The intimacy of conjugal life, begun by a confused mutual attraction, will reveal to them more and more that each needs the other to become fully human, to enrich his particular gifts by their complements; the analytical thought (sometimes too logical and abstract) of the one, complements intuitions of the other; the vigour of the first fits the delicacy and grace of his inseparable companion. While remaining individual, they fuse into one life and so discover how a person can enrich himself by giving himself, growing in love.

The man and woman who, yielding to the impulse of nature, become, in the words of the Bible, one flesh, join at the same time their personalities and become one soul. They share an experience which, whatever they may do, marks their personalities deeply and ties them together, not only by an enduring memory but by a mutual impregnation of their moral being as well as of their physical being.

Because the whole soul permeates the entire body, the fleshly union between man and woman involves and marks their souls. The blossoming of their personality is connected in a sense with the blossoming of their sexual life. Indeed, we may say that they fulfil themselves in each other and by each other in the same act which makes them one flesh. All we have said of the interlocking of the physical and the spiritual in man, of the psychosomatic unity of human life, leads to the conclusion that the act which joins the sexes is a true symbiosis. To become a father, to become a mother, each by the other, what an experience, what an enrichment for those who live these moments with a conscience illumined by love!

Then the words of Paul, apostle of Christ, become understandable when he says that the human couple symbolises magnificently the union of Christ with the gathering of believers: the *Ecclesia*. 'You who are husbands must show love to your wives, as Christ showed love to the Church when he gave himself up on its behalf. He would hallow it, purify it by bathing it in the water to which his word gave life; he would summon it into his own presence, the Church in all its beauty, no stain, no wrinkle, no such disfigurement; it was to be holy, it was to be spotless. And that is how husband ought to love wife, as if she were his own body; in loving his wife, a man is but loving himself. It is unheard of, that a man should bear ill-will to his own flesh and blood; no, he keeps it fed and warmed; and so it is with Christ and his Church.'

Here then is marriage, the symbol of the redeeming love of Christ for humanity. But is it not also the most human school of sacrifice? For love of his wife and children man forgoes selfish pleasure and prefers to seek his joy in the happiness of those he loves. For them he will discipline himself to the monotony of a regular job, he will deprive himself, suffer and will not hesitate to give his life to save them. As for mothers, it is not possible to speak of their self-sacrifice without a deep and sincere emotion.

And so into the obscure urges of sexuality the liberty and the heroism of love insinuate themselves; grace completes and surpasses nature; desire changes into tenderness; *eros* becomes *agape*.

What does it matter if the first fires of passion in marriage are calmed or even extinguished? A continual tenderness, a mutual and profound understanding expressed in a simple glance, in a discreet smile; support, consolation, encouragement, peaceful joy in the unity of hearts: these fruits are far more valuable.

Now at last one can understand that a successful conjugal life cannot countenance either instability or promiscuity. It demands the complete sharing in an involvement for life. It excludes the provisional and conditional; it excludes any looking back or after-thoughts, any sharing of the conjugal experience with someone else.

The reasons of the procreation and upbringing of children are not the only ones which demand and depend on the indissolubility of marriage : in the case of definite sterility these would no longer be valid. Marriage has therefore other essential ends besides those concerning children.

This is what is explicitly recognised in the Encyclical *Casti Connubii* : ' In this reciprocal forming and per-fecting of man and wife in the interior life, and in this assiduous application to helping each other day by day that they may advance ever more and more in virtue, one can see indeed, as the Roman catechism teaches, the primary purpose of marriage, if one does not consider it as an institution destined only to the procreation and education of children, but in a wider sense a sharing in common of all life, a constant intimacy, a society.'

And the same Encyclical goes on to quote this noteworthy statement of Cardinal Bellarmine : ' The sacrament of marriage can be regarded in two ways : first, in the making, and then in its permanent state. For it is a sacrament like to that of the Eucharist, which not only when it is being conferred, but also whilst it remains, is a sacrament; for as long as the married partners are alive, so long is their union a sacrament of Christ and the Church.'

One could say that the natural end of the conjugal act is the procreation and upbringing of the children, but in the case of man the dignity of the child, as also that of the parents, demands that the conjugal act should only be performed in a permanent and indissoluble relationship of man and woman, based on the 'generous gift of his own person made to another for the whole span of life, with the help and co-operation of God' (*Casti Connubii*).

Such a gift is not confined exclusively to procreation, but includes the mutual perfecting and the happiness of the persons who are in this way totally committed to each other. To these natural objectives there is added the supernatural objective of the Sacrament which consecrates the relationship.

It must therefore be admitted that the objectives of human, and more especially of Christian marriage are multiple and normally inseparable. Before procreation there must inevitably be the meeting, the choice, the reciprocal gift of two beings who undertake to love and cherish each other throughout life 'for better, for worse, for richer, for poorer, in sickness and in health, till death do us part.'

Such a choice, such an undertaking is not simply concerned with procreation. But on the other hand the union between man and woman tends biologically towards procreation and finds in the children which it engenders a consecration and a fulfilment of which each feels the need.

Since the experience of an integral married life includes children and certainly cannot exclude them, procreation is therefore a fundamental objective and cannot positively be discounted from the time that husband and wife become one flesh.

It could be said that the objective of marriage is to grow and perfect human nature by the union of man and woman in the family which they found, increase and govern in the interests of the good and the progress of each and all of its members. And in the specific case of Christians who acquire the sacramental grace of matrimony, it can be said that its objective is to grow and to perfect the mystical body of Christ by the union of man and woman in the family which they found, increase and govern in the interests of the spiritual well-being of each of its members.

Thus, all the immanent objectives of the state of matrimony are found to be joined and safeguarded in a perfect subordination to the final ends of man.

---

[1] Denis de Rougemont, *L'Amour et l'Occident,* Paris 1939, p. 23 (englished as *Passion and Society,* London, revised ed. 1956).

[2] I Timothy, 4, 2–5.

[3] Genesis, 1, 27; 2, 24; Matthew, 19, 4–6.

[4] *Summa,* II–IIae, q. 153, a. 2 c.

[5] *De Malo,* q. 15, a. 1.

[6] Genesis, 2, 18–25.

The Indissolubility of Marriage

Gustave Thibon

We do not intend to examine in detail the teaching
in Catholic theology on the indissolubility of marriage.
We assume that this teaching is known to our readers
and, while not omitting to recall its outlines, we will
concentrate on stressing the psychological and 'existential' aspect of the problem. On this point, as on
many others, Catholicism, which has a theology and
moral code as complete as they are balanced, has not
perhaps made a sufficient effort to justify its principles
on the plane of psychological experience and to reply
to these critics who reproach it precisely on the
grounds that it misunderstands the man of body and
soul and the concrete facts of his existence.

LET NOT MAN PUT ASUNDER

The principle of the indissolubility of marriage is
contained in its entirety in this text of the gospel:
'Then the Pharisees came to him, and put him to the
test by asking, Is it right for a man to put away his
wife, for whatever cause?' He answered, 'Have you

never read, how he who created them when they first
came to be, created them male and female; and how
he said, A man, therefore, will leave his father and
mother and will cling to his wife, and the two will
become one flesh? And so they are no longer two,
they are one flesh; what God, then, has joined, let
not man put asunder.' [1] And Saint Paul, echoing the
teaching of our Lord, puts it in this way : ' For those
who have married already, the precept holds which
is the Lord's precept, not mine; the wife is not to leave
her husband; if she has left him, she must either
remain unmarried or go back to her own husband
again, and the husband is not to put away his wife.' [2]

This requirement of indissolubility is founded on
two principles.

Firstly, *on the natural law.* Procreation, which according to the traditional doctrine is the main purpose
of marriage, cannot among human-kind be abandoned
to the hazards of a meeting-without-future, as it is
among animals. A child not only needs to be brought
into the world and suckled during the first months
of his life; his long upbringing demands the continual
presence of his father and mother, for he can only
develop fully in the centre of a united and stable
family. Therefore the separation of husband and wife,
these two cornerstones of the family edifice, necessarily
compromises the proper upbringing of children and,
as a consequence, the equilibrium of society itself.

Secondly, *on the sacramental character of marriage,*
the union of man and woman is as inseparable as
that of Christ and the Church which serves as its

prototype and its model. The couple 'which is one flesh' must tend by its fidelity to sacramental grace to become a single soul, and man has not the right to separate that which God has joined.

Founded in this way on a fundamental requirement of nature and on divine consecration, the indissolubility of marriage does not permit of any exception. The Catholic Church never pronounces a decree of divorce; she limits herself in a certain number of carefully determined cases (unconsummated marriage, lack of consent, mistaken identity, consanguinity, etc.) to confirming the nullity of the sacramental bond. All she can do in this respect is to dispel an error and an illusion; the sacrament administered in the absence of the conditions necessary to its validity is binding neither on the Church which confers it nor on the faithful who receive it, and in such cases the religious authorities, far from consenting to separate those whom God has truly joined, have merely the power of untying an illusory knot: in other words, of restoring to the apparently married a liberty which in fact they have never lost. It is not legally correct to speak of divorce where there has never been a true marriage.

GOOD REASONS FOR THE INDISSOLUBILITY OF MARRIAGE

It has often been said before that the union between man and woman, consecrated by marriage, serves two ends.

Firstly, it allows the physical and moral blossoming forth of the two who make up the couple. 'And the Lord God said : It is not good for man to be alone; let us make him a help like unto himself.' Man and woman are two complementary beings; they are made to live, not only together, but one for the other, and their mutual love and the fusion of their destinies serves both their material security and their spiritual development. Marriage constitutes at once the most elementary form and the most indestructible foundation of all social life.

Secondly, by procreation it ensures the continuity of the human species, and by the influence of the family circle it ensures the healthy upbringing of the children.

These two ends of marriage are closely linked. On the one hand the mutual attraction which joins the two sexes has procreation as a normal consequence. ' One does not marry ', said Chesterton, ' because the world needs to be peopled; one marries because one is in love.' Doubtless, but the commandment ' Increase and multiply ' is already contained in embryo in the feeling of lovers for each other. And similarly procreation, by creating new bonds between husband and wife, gives them new reason to love and help one another.

It appears, however — in so far as one can separate two elements so closely knit in the unity of real life — that it is on the first point that the Church has decided to lay the stress when she proclaims the irrevocability of marriage. Traditional theology strongly asserts that procreation is the first end of marriage, and that the mutual love of the couple takes second place. It is illuminating to notice that no other emotional relationship, no other social tie whatever its depth or spirituality, is sanctified and crowned by a sacrament. The ties which join friend and friend, a prince and his people, etc., are neither sacraments nor irrevocable; one can even where necessary, with difficulty, be released from religious vows, but not from the vows of marriage. The outstanding importance which the Church attaches to the conjugal bond demonstrates above all that she sees in it the immediate source of the natural and supernatural life of the couple, as well as the necessary foundation of human society. The words of the Scriptures leave no doubt on this point : ' The two shall be one *flesh*.' Now, what does the word ' flesh ' mean here unless it is used in the biblical sense : 'A person represented and manifested by the external appearance of our humanity '?[3]

Or, as we would say in modern terms, one single fleshly being, one single moral being. This does not mean one soul, one spirit. Spiritual union is held up as a duty and an ideal; but the simple union contracted by the exchange of consent, even without love, is sufficient to make a marriage valid and to make the tie indissoluble. But this tie is not without reference to the flesh, since the impotence of one of the parties causes the marriage to be automatically annulled, for any non-consummated marriage may be dissolved according to the decision of the Supreme Pontiff, in favour of a greater spiritual good.

But basically, what constitutes the very special nature of the marriage tie is its mysterious participation in the indissoluble union between Christ and the Church. To the extent that a very imperfect participation in this union is vouchsafed to the heathen, their legitimate marriage may be dissolved (an instance of this is the Pauline privilege); but the total participation in the nuptial mystery which is the ratified and consummated union of two Christians renders their state absolutely unalterable during the liftetime of the two partners.

It will be seen that in any case it is neither absence of love nor ' incompatibility of temperament ' that is taken into consideration by the ecclesiastical judiciary to determine the validity of the tie and its degree of indissolubility. This is because the Church, ruling the impulses and romantic sensibilities of the individual. from a lofty height, sees in marriage something more than passionate and sentimental intercourse between two people. Her care stretches beyond the ephemeral couple to the whole of the temporal City which is the body of the divine City. Husband and wife, by joining together, are not merely binding themselves to each other; they are one and the other bound to a reality which contains and surpasses them : first to the family of which they are the origin and mainstay, then to the City and the Church, a living organism of which families are the cells. Such a fundamental institution needs protection against the thousand vicissitudes of instinct and self-interest. If the couple have not the right to separate, it is less in their function as

a couple than as a link on which everything depends.
Marriage constitutes the irreducible unit of the human
community : if it breaks society crumbles. The road
on which a couple is starting out goes in only one
direction — the path of earthly life itself. The only
exit is ahead, and it is not possible to draw back
without crashing dangerously against other persons
who are being drawn in the same irreversible direction.
A marriage is dependent in the first place on the
individual; later the individual is dependent on marriage. Everyone is free to choose his own bond
according to his inclination and his will, but having
chosen it, he is no longer free to break it.

COMPANIONS FOR ETERNITY?

Institutions are to people what the bed of a river is
to its waters. The Church, in her eternal wisdom
coupled with the experience of centuries, knows well
that if such an impetuous and erratic current as
that of physical passion is not to deviate from its
course and become lost in swamps, it needs a deep
and solid foundation. This foundation is found in
marriage, both as an institution and as a sacrament.
And it is on this formal and social element of the
conjugal tie that classical theology has put the accent.
Today, in reaction, we find growing up a kind of
mystique about marriage which is preoccupied more
with the quality of the personal link between husband
and wife than with its social preservation. The ten-

dency is to see the essence of marriage more and more in the act of love, consecrated by God, thanks to which two beings join and mingle their destinies. The rest — fidelity to each other, procreation and up-bringing of children, social position, etc. — flows from this source as the temporal flows from the eternal. This is the myth of ' companions for eternity '.

Since man is formed of flesh and spirit, of individual as well as social elements, these two conceptions of marriage seem more complementary than opposite. It is good to give men a highly spiritual ideal of marriage. But on the other hand, if only to prevent a dangerous exaltation being followed by bitter dis-illusion, it is desirable to distinguish clearly between what is *essential* in marriage and what is its *perfection*. Certainly it is eminently desirable for the partners to form spiritual links deep enough to transform them into companions for eternity; but it is none the less true that such level of spirituality is not exacted as absolutely necessary to a marriage. The conjugal union as such takes place in time; and the graces attached to it, although proceeding from the divine source and striving towards eternal life, are given not only in time but for time. Independent of all the spiritual super-structures which can be added in the conscience of the people involved, the indissolubility of marriage is essentially bound up with sexuality and procreation, as objective faculties assumed through the grace of Christ, who desires to bring his eternal Body of Humanity to a state of grace. The purpose of the indissolubility of marriage is connected with the enduring quality of the Church, the body of Christ, much more than, or at least as much as, with the eternity of the individual. The fact that a marriage entered into without love is quite valid in the eyes of the Church[4] is already sufficient proof of this. And the legitimacy of second marriages shows even more clearly the temporal and social character of the indissolubility of marriage. The sacramental tie in effect is dissolved by the death of one partner, and the surviving one, released from all obligations, is free to contract a new union. Husband and wife, *as such,* are to so small an extent companions for eternity that all ties are dissolved at the very moment one individual leaves this life to enter into eternal life.

This breaking of the conjugal tie at death is clearly affirmed in the gospel: 'On that day, too, he was approached with a question by the Sadducees, men who say that there is no resurrection; Master, they said, Moses told us, if a man leaves no children when he dies, his brother shall marry the widow by right of kinship, and beget children in the dead brother's name. We had seven brothers once in our country, of whom the first died, a married man without issue, bequeathing his wife to the second. And the same befell the second brother, and then the third, and in the end all seven, the woman dying last of all. And now, when the dead rise again, which of the seven will be her husband, since she was wife to them all? Jesus answered them, You are wrong; you do not understand the scriptures, or what is the power of God. When the dead rise again there is no marrying or giving in marriage; they are as the angels in heaven are.' [5]

As to the permissibility of a second marriage, Saint Paul's position is quite clear : ' As for a wife, she is yoked to her husband as long as he lives; if her husband is dead, she is free to marry anyone she will.'[6] Speaking of widows, he says : ' So I would have the younger woman marry and bear children and have households to manage.' [7]

I have often noticed that this doctrine, which limits the sacrament in time and by death, appears to shock those in love. ' Can it be true', some couples cry, ' that beyond the tomb nothing will remain of this love which we feel will last for eternity ? ' This is the place to repeat the words of the gospel : that which is born of the flesh is flesh, and that which is born of the spirit is spirit. The Church has instituted a sacrament which is available to all. But this sacrament, properly considered, is one thing, and the quality of soul of those who receive it is another. Marriage does not necessarily confer spiritual love; but neither does it exclude it. On the contrary, indeed, the intimacy of married life and fidelity to the sacramental grace offer a soil which is particularly appropriate for the birth and blossoming of such a love. ' They are as the angels in heaven are ', said Christ. Everything angelic, that is, truly spiritual, which we have put into our love, will be preserved in heaven. Death dissolves marriage in the physical and social sense (is it, alas, anything else for most couples ?); it does not dissolve the spiritual friendship which fuses together two immortal souls. It is exclusively in this sense that we can speak of companions for eternity. Whatever is immortal in marriage surpasses marriage; at death, the union of the couple, broken below and transfigured above, becomes an aspect of the communion of saints.

OBJECTIONS TO THE INDISSOLUBILITY OF MARRIAGE

If there are those who, spurred on by an untimely thirst for the ideal, are inclined to reproach the Church for limiting the indissolubility to life on earth, and for allowing second marriages, there are far more who accuse her of being unjustifiably rigid because she forbids divorce. Both of these criticisms proceed from the same source : the revolt of subjective inclinations against a universal law. Not realising that an institution such as marriage is made first and foremost in the interests of mankind as a whole, the former want to shape it according to their faithfulness, and the latter according to their inconstancy, but in both cases there is the desire to make the law according to the individual.

The opponents of the indissolubility of marriage rely chiefly on the following arguments :

The Church, they say, shows an inhuman inflexibility in this matter. She fails to recognise the aspirations and most permissible rights of the individual. By prolonging until death marriages which have been contracted without love, or from which love has faded away, she is sacrificing the reality for the appearance, the inner kernel for the social husk, the living person for an unfeeling law. A union has no value unless it is quickened by love; and when two people have nothing left of the intimate ties of love and only the exterior fetters of the law remain, there is no longer any real marriage. Why then persist in preserving what is already dead? This is but a process of embalming which is contrary to the natural law.

The law of the Church, by forbidding an estranged couple to rebuild their lives on the basis of a new love, impedes or prevents the exercise of the most noble of man's faculties; for either the individual who is obedient to the law kills this new love in embryo and lives in an emotional desert, or else he violates the law, whereupon his love, regarded as sinful and condemned by morality and public opinion, of necessity leads a shameful and mutilated existence.

All this — the hypocrisy of pretending to a legal love or hiding a true but illegitimate love — smacks of a pharisaical atmosphere which is eminently unfavourable to the virtue of individuals and the well-being of society.

And as for the social advantages which are set forth to the credit of the indissolubility of marriage, do they not find their negative counterpart in this primacy of the abstract over the concrete, the letter over the spirit, in this cult of ' virtue ' emptied of body and soul and reduced to the most formal skeleton, which sets society in an atmosphere of constraint and lies, and in its turn prepares destructive attacks of revolt and anarchy? Has it not been in reaction against a too exacting conformity that the worst offences have come? And as for the Church — which already allows physical separation — would it not be in her interest to allow free play in some cases to this safety-valve called divorce?

To sum up, nothing is gained by trying to yoke a complex and moving life to an abstract and rigid law: the only result is to make the law sterile and to poison the life.

In replying to these criticisms we will be neither so foolish or hypocritical as to refuse to see the measure of truth which they contain. Of all human attributes, love between man and woman is the one which requires that the most disparate elements should be adjusted in order to ensure its harmonious development. The life of the couple constitutes in effect the point of convergence of the most diverse needs — and sometimes the most opposed ones — of human nature: the need for physical and spiritual fulfilment of *both* the people involved, procreation and upbringing of children, social requirements, moral and religious ideals, etc. It is obvious that the most successful issue in this matter will always be somewhat imperfect. The law of mingling and of relativity, which is the central law of creation, is the foundation of this refuge for our earthly life which is marriage. Similarly the principle which should guide us through this maze is not that of absolute perfection: it is that of the greatest good, not to say that of the least evil. And,

taken all in all, we find it in the doctrine of the indissolubility of marriage.

LAW AND LIFE

Only in our own time have the deep contacts which
exist between sensibility and the mind been recognised;
it has resulted in an undeniable enlargement of psychological knowledge. But this victory has it price. Modern
thought, centred on existentialism and subjectivism,
tends more and more to fail to recognise or to ignore
everything in our nature and our destiny which holds
out against the onslaught of living experience and
psychological analysis. Laws, institutions — human or
divine — are the first victims of this state of mind.
We forget that they have an existence, a dignity of
their own, independent of the people involved, and
we judge their value — indeed their legitimacy —
solely by their evident psychological effects, their existential resonance. And if these effects are not seen,
if the sounding of souls does not permit us to observe
these resonances, the institution is despised.

Applied to sacramental marriage, this method gives
rise to the following argument. ' What God then has
joined. . . This sacrament is great. . . ' Such words
express the ideal essence of marriage. But how much
remains in real life? Where are the effects of such a
great sacrament in the souls of those innumerable
husbands and wives, united only by instinct, self-
interest and habit, who enter into marriage and never

come out, remaining in a rut for all their life? Conclusion: where love is not lived from the inside, there is no marriage. The great existentialist, Nietzsche, has taken up this subjective concept of marriage in a strongly worded aphorism: 'They say that their unions have been sealed in heaven. But I have no use for this unnecessary God who comes limping to bless what he has not united.'

What he has not united . . . the word appears to go far: in fact, it does not go beyond man and his subjective outlook. What God has not united on the level of individual experience he may well have united on another level. Every institution which aims directly at the lives of persons, and at the maintenance of their ultimate orientation, that is, the conjugal community and the ecclesiastical community, transcends persons, or at least identifies itself with the individual's transcendance. The attitude of Saint Thomas on this point disposes of any loophole. On the question of whether a marriage contracted for an 'ignoble' reason (for example, physical desire alone, or material interest) constitutes a true marriage, he replies that such a union is perfectly valid, although the one who contracts it is, as a consequence, in a state of sin. And to critics who put forward the objection that marriage, which is a good thing in itself and the earthly reflection of the union between Christ and the Church, cannot legally proceed from an impure cause, he answers that marriage is one thing and the motives of those who contract it are another.[8] It is not possible to make a clearer distinction between the institution and the subjective inclinations of the individual. In the social edifice, the individuals are the stones and the institutions are the cement. Today, many of the stones complain of being held by the cement without feeling its effect within themselves : they feel that they are the only ones in the edifice. But the cement nevertheless protects the building's existence and stability. And if every stone, rebelling against this inhuman cement which holds it without penetrating it, asserted its individual freedom, the most obvious result of this demand for ' the rights of the individual' would be the collapse of the building.[9]

You admit then, the adversary will retort triumphantly, that the sacrament of marriage has no other significance than as a social and religious setting, and that it remains, by its own nature, radically opposed to love. In that case why not follow your line of reasoning to its conclusion and admit, with the troubadours, that marriage and love are mutually exclusive, since the first implies obligation and constraint, while the second is intrinsically spontaneous and free?

Before coming to grips with the argument, let us examine more closely that which hides too often under the fine name of love. People are scandalised to see that the Church contents herself with a simple voluntary agreement, even one dictated by the most unworthy motives, to chain two beings together for ever. On the contrary, this course seems to us to be full of wisdom, and the findings of modern psychology (exploration of the subconscious, criticism of ideals, exposure of self-deception, etc.) fully justifies it. The

Church is accused of sacrificing love, the inner reality, to the institution, the social appearance. But, apart from the fact that the Church cannot undertake to define the validity of a permanent and universal institution in the moving tide of subjective dispositions and accidental causes she would have to be quite sure that the love argument would always result in social order. Genuine love is rare, and its caricatures are numerous. La Rochefoucauld has already said that ' love lends its name to an infinite number of trans-actions with which it is no more concerned than the Doge is with what takes place in Venice.' ' Sincerity ' in this respect does not count for a great deal; too often it is nothing more than the art of lying spontan-eously and to oneself. How many men believe they love, while their love is composed only of physical lust, and illusory exaltation, and a greedy desire to conquer and dominate! Is such a love not even more unreal than an institution? Is passion, briefly hotter and more intoxicating than the law, any less illusory for all that? I refer to all those who have never raised a barrier to their freedom of loving : the ashes which the straw-fires of former passions have left in their hearts will suffice to show them the emptiness of free love. Comparing the one with the other, the law which ensures the continuation of the human species and the equilibrium of society is at least worth as much as the passion which ensures only a temporary selfish happiness for the individual.

But all that is said only to defeat the adversary on his own ground, for it is not true that law is only an external thing, nor that it is contrary to love. All that we can concede to our adversaries is that the sacrament of marriage does not confer love. In the same way that the sacrament of penance makes contrition more effective, but does not necessarily supply it, so the sacrament of marriage crowns and perfects the conjugal vows, but does not supply out of nothing what is lacking. It is like this with the supernatural in all its forms : *gratia supponit et perficit naturam* (grace presupposes and perfects nature). Just to arrive at the altar is not enough to ensure mutual consent, still less love; nature herself can supply consent and love; and grace, which is of another order, operates on another plane. It is more to the point for each to examine himself and to decide for himself if he is enough in love to betake himself to the altar. But, this point once decided, the indissolubility of marriage, far from being opposed to love, is in fact on its side.

Before marriage, first of all. The sole fact of knowing that the contract which he is about to undertake is irrevocable, incites the individual not to venture lightly into this impasse where the gates shut behind him. To take the image of a conqueror who, before the battle, cuts off all possibility of retreat by burning his boats, the engaged couple who agree to be bound together until death obtain through this ' idea of necessity ' a preliminary guarantee against all the future hazards of fate which will threaten their love. On the other hand, the mere idea of a *possible* divorce would lurk cunningly in the depths of the soul like a worm, which settles down and is likely one day to devour the substance. Has it not sometimes been said, particularly at times of great stress, that it is sufficient to see a thing as possible for it to become necessary? This elementary psychological fact is enough to wipe out the notion of 'trial marriage', suggested by some reformers of marriage who are more concerned with inventing paradoxes than with basing them on solid arguments.

Then after marriage. The marriage contract, by settling once and for all the substance of love above all contingencies, must of necessity help to purify this love. The fact of having to undergo and surmount the test of time works on the affection of the couple like a sieve which separates the chaff from the grain : it gradually strips it of its accidental and illusory elements in order to retain only the uncorruptible kernel. It transforms passion into true love. But, what if there is no love at the beginning, the adversary will argue? We will answer by repeating that if the duty of fidelity can change nothing of the intrinsic quality of this delicate fruit which is love, it at least creates a climate which, by eliminating the dangers of a stunted development, guides it to a happy maturity. For love is not given or refused us by the whim of an unalterable decree; like all living things it undergoes an evolution by means of tests, crises and illnesses. Threatened from the inside by habit and from the outside by the attractiveness of change, it can, according to the way it reacts to these tests, either emerge strengthened, or die. ' Everything that does not kill me makes me stronger ', said

Nietzsche. And in just the same way the Church, by imposing on love the obligation not to die, helps to transform these crises and illnesses by a purifying process whereas, in a less rigorous climate these crises would result in death. The principle of the indissolubility of marriage puts time — this touchstone of reality — at the service of love.

It is nevertheless true that some unions show a total and incurable deadlock on the level of human love. We all know couples who, as the result of complete incompatibility of feelings, have not the least hope of putting the slightest thread of understanding and tenderness into the inexorable chain which binds them until death. We are forced to admit that in such cases indissoluble marriage does appear to be an inhuman law. Why are these unfortunates obliged to drag along all through their lives the results of a sudden and often involuntary mistake — and why should one action, perhaps the most ridiculous of their lives, be a permanent stumbling-block to their future?

Let us arrange our answer.

It can happen first of all that these regrettable unions have valid grounds for annulment (madness of one of the partners, lack of consent, etc.). This solution settles everything.

But if this is not the case, that is to say, if these psychologically catastrophic unions fulfil the formal conditions for a true marriage, the answer is as plain as it is hard: the Church commands these ' unloved ones ' and these unsuitably joined persons to renounce utterly all expectation of love and human happiness.

But to what does she sacrifice them? Quite simply to the common good, which, where compromise is not possible, must always be put before the good of the individual. The principle of indissoluble marriage is like a gate attacked by the tempest of passions and personal interests: if it is half-opened, it is no longer possible to keep it on its hinges, and the entire hurricane will engulf everything. The victims of marriage deserve all possible sympathy, but not that exceptions should be made in their favour, for one exception leads to another (in effect, are not all human situations exceptional in that they are unique and cannot be paralleled?) and so the rule which is the main beam of the social edifice is destroyed. Also, this require-ment of personal sacrifice for the general welfare is found not only in marriage. Other institutions, other social realities demand the same individual denial of self. If it seems a scandal that an estranged couple should have to bury their personal happiness for the sake of a universal institution which protects the hap-piness of others, what about the soldier who is asked by his country to die in order to save this national well-being in which he will not share? Contradictions like these are part of our human lot, and it has not been until this period of morbid hyperaesthesia of self, and crass insistence on personal rights, that the happi-ness of the individual is thought of as an *unconditional* right and these contradictions regarded as matter for indignation and scandal.

And then, are these unlucky couples permanently banned from the blessings of love and joy? The very

barrier which prevents human happiness can lead
them to seek higher for a purer happiness. When a
road on earth is closed before and behind there is
only one way out : the sky. There was a time when
merely human loyalties were enough to sustain en-
thusiasm and faithfulness : it is thus, for example,
that it was possible to serve until death a prince whom
one disliked, from pure faithfulness to the institution
of monarchy. One saw in him, more than the person
he was, the representative of a protective tradition,
the link in a chain which joined the past to the future.
But if monarchy does not peter out in the person of
the prince, with still more reason the marriage tie
goes beyond the persons concerned. As a human
institution, marriage links past generations to the generations to come, and as a sacrament it fastens us to
eternity. *What God has joined* : in extreme cases it
is on the word *God* that one must lay the stress, and
this unity, lost on earth, must be sought for in heaven.
Above the marriage partner whom it is impossible to
love, there is always the person of God *who is love,*
and what miscarries in time can always blossom in
eternity.

As for the accusation of hypocrisy which is so prone
to be levelled at a husband and wife who stay together
without love, and whose whole virtue seems to lie in
' keeping up appearances ', it calls for a double re-
assessment. First of all, appearances do have a value :
on the one hand they constitute the framework of
society and as well as this they ensure, rather in the
manner of paper money, the continuity and harmony

of exterior relations among men. Pascal has already said, with a deep wisdom very different from that of the apostles of sincerity-at-all-costs, that without respect for conventions and the ' rules of the game ' no social life would be possible. Secondly, it would be a good idea to define clearly what is meant by the words hypocrisy and sincerity. To be sincere is to show openly what one is inside. Very well. But then wherever there is duality and conflict, wherever man is called upon to choose between a desire and a duty, there is in one sense hypocrisy. Are we going to accuse of insincerity the thirsty traveller who, passing under a tree belonging to someone else, refrains from picking the fruit his thirst craves? Or the soldier who goes up to the assault when the desire of his whole being is to run away and to survive? It is just the same for those couples who remain faithful to the obligations of a marriage without love. If all that represents a victory over self is called hypocrisy, what then is sincerity? Must one, under the excuse of being true to oneself, follow all one's impulses and put all one's desires into action? Surely the fickleness and betrayal which are the unavoidable results of this principle, are lies which are just as deep as and infinitely more destructive than artificial faithfulness? Inasmuch as man has not obtained perfect inner unity he is condemned to hypocrisy, in the etymological sense of the word (hypo = below), that is to say, he has to dissemble, to push back into obscurity and silence part of himself. Only the brute and the saint do not experience inner conflict, and, wholly involved in their actions, they thus completely escape from hypocrisy, the one basely, for he is but instinct, the other sublimely, for he is but love.

To sum up, on whatever ground the argument is based, the indissolubility of marriage gives more advantages than disadvantages. Wherever the union is psychologically real, that is to say, based on love, it protects and deepens this love. Wherever it is psychologically unreal, that is to say, deprived of love, it at least saves the social reality of marriage. Thus, if it cannot always realise the best, at least it avoids the worst.

THE PROBLEM OF 'FREE' LOVE

There is, however, one case where the principle of indissolubility of marriage seems to be opposed to love : where incompatible marriage partners are forbidden by the Church to enter into a new union and pushed out of her communion, as 'public sinners', if they dare to brave the forbidden barrier. Is an institution not barbarous when it labels as 'clandestine' — with all that that word evokes of shame and suffering — the most sincere affections, which in a less severe climate could blossom in full daylight?

This is the objection in all its force. We can reply, without any suspicion of paradox, that even on this point the inflexibility of the Church still serves true love — in so far as it condemns false love.

Let us explain. We are not so naive as to pretend that love can be found only in marriage. First of all it is obvious that love which leads to marriage begins before marriage (one does not love because one marries, one marries because one loves). And, even outside marriage, true love can be found : nobody will argue, for example, that the sin of Heloise and Abelard did not hold more human fulfilment than a legitimate union contracted solely out of material motives or by the inert force of habit. But great passions and, even more so, great loves are exceedingly rare.[10] It is too easy to denounce the emptiness of certain marriages where under a veil of social respectability crawl the most despicable passions or the most incurable mediocrity. But why not show the other side of the picture ? If great loves are rare within marriage, are they so very frequent outside it ? Let the detractors of marriage consider for a moment the quality of most free relationships : they will have little difficulty in finding there all the faults of a bad marriage, with the addition of a revolt against social order and religious law. The Church is absolutely right to maintain the unity of the family and the health of the community against the destructive assaults of individual passions which subjectively are worth no more than the worst marriages and objectively gnaw at the foundations of the common good. Marriage does not exclude, alas, either the violence of instinct or greed or selfishness but it does at least give them orbits and bounds. But the anarchic passion which, under the guise of love, conceals the avaricious claims of the flesh and self without any directive truly deserves no leniency.

As for the great unlawful love — that which compels with all the force of inevitability, and which involves one's whole being — Catholic morality offers two solutions: either to go beyond the law by sacrificing the fleshly and earthly side of the affection and sublimating it entirely to the ideal region where love has no law other than its own, or else to break the law openly with all the responsibilities, all the risks and all the suffering which are the consequence of this action.

The *normal* duties of marriage (procreation, bringing up of the children, mutual fidelity of husband and wife) do not exhaust *a priori* and in all cases the sexual tendency of the human being: this tendency permeates also the high regions of the soul and marks our immortal being. A man or woman may thus sometimes find outside marriage his true companion for eternity. Love blows where it wills: Beatrice was not the wife of Dante, Holderlin did not marry Diotima. The most exacting morality does not demand that such a love should be killed in embryo, but rather that it should be placed high above time and the flesh so that, no longer a threat to the order and well-being protected by the law, it will no longer have to suffer because of the law's strictness. Here let us be continually on our guard against mere romantic imaginings, and let us stress once more the exceptional character of these sublimated great loves. Outside marriage the woman is more often Delilah than Beatrice, and the being in whom we hope to find ' the eternal feminine which leads us upwards ' is very likely to be in reality but Eve led astray by the serpent who drags us down in her fall. . .

As for the free union as such — where the lovers do not fear to infringe the law — we do not deny that it can encompass, beside a serious moral lapse, a higher quality of love. Well! Even on this ground, which is precisely that of the adversary, we dare to state that the exigencies of the Christian law contribute yet again to enhance the quality of that love. Let us not be afraid to become for a moment the devil's advocate : we are still pleading for God, because whatever good remains in the devil always comes from God! It is just that whoever violates the law should suffer the repercussions of his rebellion. Without going so far as to endorse the Spanish proverb : ' Do what you like, pay the price and God will be happy ', we feel that he who accepts all the consequences of his sin carries already within himself the seed of deliverance and pardon. ' Be either hot or cold. . . .' If the Prodigal Son, having left his father, had placed his capital in gilt-edged securities and indulged in prudent debauches, he would doubtless never have returned to the house of his birth. There is something worse than sin : it is the fraudulent desire to win both sides while playing only one hand — the wish to enjoy the pleasures of sin and the advantages of virtue, to want the drunkenness of anarchy and the benefits of an orderly existence. In this game all that remains noble and deep in sin evaporates instantly. And it is precisely for this reason that the intransigence of the Church serves free love indirectly, not certainly *insofar as it is free,* but *insofar as it is love.* She limits it as regards number, she deepens it as regards the quality : a double advantage. By imposing on the candidates for sin strong barriers to surmount and bitter suffering to bear, she makes a selection among unruly passions and raises the level of those which stand the test. Indeed it must never be forgotten that everything is contained in man and that at whatever period or in whatever society it may arise, the quality of sin depends on the quality of virtue : only good wine makes good vinegar. Purity and the stability of the marriage institution purge and consolidate free love; it is by virtue of the obstacles opposed to it by a healthy morality that anarchic passion conserves some force and greatness. The human value and energy of a breaker of boundaries depends on the strength of those boundaries : neither strength nor courage is necessary to force an open door. Similarly it has been at a period when the principle of the indissolubility of marriage did not permit of any exception that the truly great unlawful passions flourished, whether in a legend like that of Tristan and Isolde, or in real life, as in the case of Abelard and Heloise. But wherever free love is practised without restriction, wherever adultery and divorce do not come under the strictures of the law or of public opinion : where are those great adventurers of love worthy of attracting attention and of causing tears to flow for generations to come? Where there are no longer any risks there is no more adventure. Unlawful love becomes commonplace if there is no element of tragedy. When Tristan and Isolde, instead of wandering through the inhospitable forest, sustained by their love alone, consummate their adultery in middle-class comfort, without danger or punishment, they will no longer arouse the slightest interest. Ease corrupts everything, including disorder. The worst disgrace that can befall sin is to be placed within the reach of all. Where there are no more forbidden fruits only rotten fruits remain.

To conclude: there are in free love elements of love and of freedom. The first is the fruit, the second the worm. The law of the Church, by imposing limits and restrictions on this devouring freedom, protects the substance of the fruit against the ravages of the worm.

A GRAIN OF WHEAT MUST FALL
INTO THE GROUND AND DIE. . .

There was a time when institutions carried individuals along: man believed in them voluntarily and made his destiny flow in the mould offered to him by laws and customs.

In our 'reflex age', on the contrary, it is the individuals who support institutions: man does not consent to obey them except insofar as, reclothed by a sort of interior consecration, they respond to a subjective need, to his personal choice.

This attitude has its negative side as well as its positive side. It constitutes a terrible threat to the stability of institutions, but it tends at the same time to eliminate social and religious conformism. In periods where disorder penetrates into customs, obedience to the law becomes the expression of love and liberty.

It is usual to bemoan the hardness of indissoluble marriage. But is it the law which is too hard for man, or is it that man is too soft for the law? To him who loves nothing all ties appear as chains. But he who knows that an everlasting love lives within him has no fear of pledging himself until death. And it is precisely to this deepening and purifying of love that the Christian law invites us. Seen from this angle, the institution of marriage appears as the guardian of inner faithfulness. As he is not made for the Sabbath, neither is man made for marriage. It is marriage which is made for man. But man is not simply an individual: he can only attain his true destiny by rising, through love and sacrifice, above the limits of his fleshly and fallen self. This is the meaning of the parable in the Gospel: a grain of wheat must fall into the ground and die. It dies, and at the same time it enters into its true life when, renouncing its selfish hardness and solitude, it begins to entrench its roots in the earth and to raise its shoot towards the sky. A perfect picture of marriage with its temporal depths and its divine consecration. . . At this level, the requirement of indissolubility mingles with the most intimate vow of the human person, for both lead us to surpass ourselves: this is the essence of love, and the dawn of eternal salvation.

[1] Matthew 19,3–6.

[2] 1 Corinthians 7, 10–11.

[3] Bonsirven, *Le Divorce dans le Nouveau Testament,* Paris 1948, p. 30.

[4] Cf Saint Thomas, *Summa,* suppl. XL, VIII, 2.

[5] Matthew 22, 23–30.

[6] 1 Corinthians 7, 39.

[7] 1 Timothy 5, 14.

[8] *Summa,* suppl. XLVIII, 2.

[9] The comparison is in some ways inadequate. In the human edifice the stones can and should be penetrated by the cement which binds them, or in other words, the institution can and should be lived within the soul; but in either case it is valid.

[10] In any case it is going too far to oppose these great passions to love. Love 'outside the pale', in the extent to which it is truly love, tends towards marriage, that is, towards the irrevocable fusion of two beings and their lives; it is a sort of marriage in spirit which the hostility of circumstances has frustrated.

The Mystery of Love

Jacques Madaule

It is difficult to speak once again of love when centuries of literature and experience seem to have exhausted the subject. It is easy enough, of course, to isolate the mystery of love, but much more difficult to discuss it. Even when we have weighed, counted and analysed in the greatest detail the reasons for the exclusive choice which one person makes of another, we feel that they are insufficient and that the essence has escaped us. The mystery of love: this is something which cannot be put into words, and which properly speaking cannot be described. Stendhal shows clearly the different stages of love after it has been born, but of its actual birth he can tell us nothing: there is nothing which he could tell us. The psychoanalysts of today will offer a wealth of advice after the event, but the thing itself, this sudden inclination of our freedom towards that of another — they cannot explain it. Why should it be he or she and no other? To this question neither the lover, nor those who observe him, can offer the least answer, unless it be the immortal words of Isolde and Tristan : ' Because it was he; because it was she.'

Love seems to make us aware of the uniqueness of a person. We quite realise that each personality is unique, that it is of infinite dimension, that it contains an image of divinity. But this knowledge is of no significance until we meet the person whose uniqueness speaks to us like a direct call. We know the platonic myth of the hermaphrodites who, when separated, would seek each other throughout the world. When they meet, the love between them makes the form of recognition. But if this is so, why is it that this recognition is not always mutual? What of him who recognises the other but is not recognised by her? One of them must be mistaken. But which one? Are we dealing with a mistaken recognition or with blindness on the part of the one who is recognised but does not in his turn recognise? However tempting the platonic myth, we must dismiss it. Bodies and souls are not formed so that this person is predestined for that one by a sort of natural affinity. And anyhow, where would our liberty be in such a case?

It is chance, and frequently the most banal chance, which seems to be responsible for these choices which so often involve destinies. Those who despise love can in vain pretend that it depends on the hour of the day and on a host of surrounding circumstances. In fact, one's personal disposition is a very important element. If I had not chanced to have such a meeting when my heart was empty, it is probable that I would not have fallen in love. We always experience a kind

F

of stupefaction in recalling the beginnings, for we find them quite insignificant in comparison with the tremendous consequences which have been their outcome. The Christian is tempted to make Providence play a part here, and good people often say that marriages are made in heaven. However, we must not read the direct intervention of God into matters of secondary causes. God permits what happens, but he does not actually will it. We can always, at least at the beginning, resist involvement. If love is not fed by a certain amount of willingness, it soon dies through lack of nourishment.

But man likes to lose his burden of liberty. There are few true lovers who do not take pleasure in the idea that they are driven by an irresistible force. This is the meaning, for example, of the myth of the love potion which Tristan and Isolde inadvertently swallowed. The terminology of the erotic poets is very characteristic in this respect also. They represent love as a child armed with a bow and arrows. How is it possible to resist this arrow which has pierced the heart? : one is no more responsible than for a wound received on the field of battle. A few precautions are not of course without value, but there are none which can promise complete invulnerability. Even strong and brave people are seen to fall like this in the evening of their life. The same poets speak of charms and captivity, which implies that from the moment when we are struck by love we have lost our freedom of movement, and even more, freedom of our feelings. They stress the physical effects of love, the pallor which is the result of the blood flowing back to the heart at the sight of the loved one; the faltering, shy speech, the impossibility of self-possession, as though the lover had fallen under a spell.

The enslavement of self is one of the most characteristic signs of love. Henceforth the centre of our interests is elsewhere. Nothing counts for us now but that unique being who is not us, and with whom we want to attain a complete identity. But this complete identification is itself impossible, and one thinks of the disillusioned words of the poet: 'We were two, I swear it.' Love at once poses the problem of communication between individuals. Can two beings communicate through everything they are and give each other all that they are? The sex act is the most intimate physical communication between two persons. It is the symbol and the sign of the closest act of communication. Each gives what is most secret and most hidden. It becomes the instrument of an intimate and mutual delight.

But it is no more than a symbol. The most intense sensuality leaves us unsatisfied, and the separateness which follows is often more bitter and absolute than that which preceeded it. Moreover, it is not just a physical matter, nor even primarily a physical matter. Through the body of the other it is the soul which we strive to reach and grasp. Hence the almost invariably violent character of the act of love. We wish to attack this beauty which attracts us and which wounds us. We want to shatter its form, to see it dissolve in this shock which we have caused. We try to conquer what has conquered us. The sensuality of a double defeat is our supreme satisfaction.

These matters are difficult to explain, but it is necessary to speak of them in order to understand one of the fundamental aspects of human love. The hope is that in the instant of a single flash all difference shall vanish; the barriers which separate the sexes and the personalities shall disappear. We have possessed as we are possessed, and in this mutual possession is the fulfilment of love. But although the entire being is involved in these acts we cannot but feel their poverty and their inadequacy. There is a part of the other which we can never reach and which is concealed from us, even while he passionately desires to give himself entirely. Similarly we are well aware that there is a part of ourselves which we can never give.

It is this which gives love its resemblance to a battle. It may be said that the two sexes challenge each other to a sort of duel where no victory and no defeat is ever final. Each keeps within himself the secret of his pleasure and cannot share it. We pass constantly from selfishness to selflessness without ever knowing which of the two is uppermost. I take and I am taken. I would not take if I had not already been taken. I have as much pleasure in being taken as in taking; and the same goes for the other in a rhythm which resembles the beat of the heart. For example, it is often asked whether it is preferable to love or to be loved. A meaningless question, for one cannot love without wishing to be loved, just as one cannot be loved without wanting to love in return.

Similarly it is a sophistry to discuss the liberty which two lovers relinquish to each other. It is clear, in effect, that what I love is the liberty of the other, and that, if she were not a free creature, to love her would be unthinkable. But I take it for granted that this liberty should be freely sacrificed to me as I freely sacrifice my liberty to her. The supreme act of liberty is self-enslavement. Love is a mutual and voluntary service. I cannot desire the other to be no longer 'other' since it is this otherness which I love. However she must wish to sacrifice her otherness to me, as I sacrifice my otherness to her. But this sacrifice is never consummated, for, if it were, it would be the end of love, or rather, at the same time its fulfilment and its death. Thus love is the pursuit of the impossible, and herein lies all its charm.

What is it in the human creature that can exert such a pull on another human being? Nature does not answer this question, and we have no choice but to resign ourselves to her silence and indifference. The being in front of me, however, can reply or not reply, and has complete liberty to do so or not to do so. My liberty makes appeal to her liberty. What is more, she is unique. Certainly there are many other women, but this one is unique for me; I am the only one to be aware of her uniqueness, and it is what is unique in me which appeals to what is unique in her. Does she feel the same need of me that I feel of her? This question which I ask myself and which I cannot

prevent myself from asking, contains all the charm
and all the tragedy of love.

She can, indeed, choose not to reply, or reply in a
way utterly different from what I would like or would
have imagined. For imagination plays an immense and
decisive role in this matter. In more than one sense
I am the creator of what I love, and what the object
of love must accept is to be more or less created by
me who loves her. This is why it is not wrong to try
to please, and it is even one of the most obvious
characteristics of love. In seeking to please I force
myself to respond to a certain need of the other; to
be as she imagines the one she loves should be. Two
people who are in love appear to one another in a
quite different light from that in which they appear
to those who are not in the secret. Hence the im-
pression that lovers are living in a dream. But nothing
is less likely to be the case, because blind love is
perhaps the only kind which sees clearly, since it is
the only one to realise a certain uniqueness.

This rather abstract account applies to what is com-
monly known as passionate love. The authorities on
love have, as everyone is aware, distinguished between
many other kinds of love, such as intellectual love,
or even conceited love. But it seems to me that when
one speaks of love without any epithet it is passionate
love that is under consideration. This kind of love, we
have amply shown, is never simple. It is linked to a
personality which is invariably complex. It is true that

physical appearance is an essential part because it is
this aspect of the personality which is seized on by our
senses. But in this physical appearance itself there are
particular traits which inspire love. We know that the
erotic poets praise chiefly the eyes and the smile of
their mistresses. The eyes, because the soul seems to
express itself mainly through them. Certain glances
speak; they betray what speech will not or cannot say;
very often they express love itself before it dares to call
itself by its proper name. By looking at someone in a
certain way we can leave her without any doubt as
to our feelings towards her. It is by means of the eyes
that the personality can go beyond the person. As for
the smile, it is even more mysterious than the glance.
Here the mouth also is a means of communication.
But the words which it produces are meagre. No-
where is one struck by the shortcomings of speech
as in the relationship of love. The smile, which is of
course not only a gesture of the mouth but also of the
eyes, says what words are incapable of saying. There
is also the demeanour, the gestures, the attractiveness
of the whole personality, and in particular the tone
of voice where, as in the eyes, soul and body inter-
mingle. This holds good to such an extent that, when
we love, these are the visible tokens which attract and
seduce us in the first place, and it is these which
continue to hold us, constantly reminding us of the
original feeling.

But indeed we cannot persuade ourselves that these
external things are merely superficial. In fact, they
are signs which point to something else, to the myster-

ious complete person. This word 'person' has been used with many different meanings. For example in Dante, Francesca de Rimini speaks of her own 'person' as follows: 'Love, which attaches itself to a generous heart . . . took my beautiful person from me.' It is of her body that she speaks. For a woman, to give her person often means to give her body. In fact, because of the way one imagines the relationship of body and soul, they are linked on earth by such a tie that we cannot give one without the other. Whoever demands the body without the soul does a terrible injury to the being which he importunes. But the injury is hardly less, although it is of quite a different character, when it is a question of demanding the soul and rejecting the body.

Perhaps it may be said that the differences between love and friendship turns precisely on this point: that friendship is purely spiritual, while love is at the same time of the flesh. This is why friendship tends to exist between two members of the same sex, while love is not so. The body of a woman attracts that of a man, and *vice versa*. But one is impelled to think that in love the souls have a kind of sex, and indeed one often hears reference to the 'feminine soul' and the 'masculine soul.' The characteristic of sex is to involve the person in its entirety. A feminine soul is no more difficult to distinguish from a masculine one than a feminine face is from a masculine face. We return to the lines of Claudel: 'It is everything in him which demands everything in the other.' Just as we cannot limit love to sex, so we cannot reduce it to the body. But sex is indispensable as is the body itself, and we may conclude by saying that love is the most complete intercommunication which can exist between two human beings.

To love is to aspire to this total communication, without excluding anything. In the case of a joyful and perfect love, every one of these attributes has a place of its own. The grace of body and face evokes in us sexual desire, and at the same time causes us to aspire to a sort of fusion and marriage of souls. Francesca was therefore not wrong in applying the word 'person' to this body which had been taken from her, because it was through it that love took hold of Paolo Malatesta and that he developed his double devotion to body and soul. But the case of the girl from Rimini is a privileged one, for she says in the next line: 'Love, which forbids that any loved one should not love.' No line is more beautiful or more true in its context. But none is more obviously false in real life. We are living in a disordered world, where not only does love permit the loved one not to love, but where it may even prevent love.

I will not dwell on the innumerable cases where love is not returned, since they are as varied as the very people who find themselves in this position. However, to be loved, without being able to love in return is, if anything, more difficult to bear. Do we find it easy to bear the love of God, this subtle and ceaseless pursuit of us by a being who is invisible and all-powerful, who only wants us to love him freely, willingly? All the efforts of ascetic and mystical theology are devoted to making us submissive and receptive to the influence of God. But the smallest distraction draws us off. Quite simply, to allow oneself to be loved one must have renounced oneself. Love which is directed towards us is a weight which we are always wanting to shake off. It seems to us to be an unbearable assault on our liberty. Whoever does not love repeats over and over to the one who loves him : ' Leave me free; your demands are intolerable.' What freedom do we mean, if it is not the freedom not to love; what demands, if not the demands of love? In order to allow myself to be loved by the other I must renounce myself completely. No creature has the right to exact for his own gain such a renunciation. But the lover cannot exact less, which is why he is so often rebuffed.

But this refusal takes many forms. Sometimes it is categorical and without appeal. But frequently it is vague, equivocal, and allows some false hope to remain. A person who refuses love but wants to ' remain good friends ' can enjoy conversation with one from whom he intends, somehow, to protect his liberty. The one who is not in love will reproach the other for her desire, which he calls base and material; he may reproach her selfishness, as if it were not just as selfish to refuse to give yourself to someone who needs you as to want the person whom you yourself need. It is a tragic dialogue between deaf people in which both are right and wrong at the same time. The flower who does not want to be plucked is amazed that just contemplating her is not enough. She calls for an impossible disinterestedness, while she herself is interested only in reserving the freedom to make another choice.

It seems to me to be very difficult to avoid these unhappy misunderstandings entirely, for, even when love is returned, it is still not exactly the same for a man as for a woman. The characteristic of each sex demands that the man tries to take, and that for him love appears as a conquest, while the woman wants to be taken and to submit passionately to the will of him whom she has chosen. Hence this jealousy which is almost inseparable from the happiest love. For no woman is so vain as to be incapable of imagining that the desire to take and to conquer, which is the property of the male, might not lead him to turn to someone else. In vain she knows herself to be unique; others are unique too, and her lover or her husband might one day notice them. It is the same for the man : this passivity to which he has reduced his companion, this helplessness in which she can refuse him nothing : could not someone else reduce her to this? And this jealousy on which love feeds is at the same time its continual torment. It is part of the duality which one cannot and would not alter. I would not love you if you were no longer yourself; but in the extent to which you are yourself you can always escape from me, so that what attaches me to you is what makes me despair.

I have considered also the very rare case of a perfect and absolute reciprocity. But it is almost never realised. One of the two was always the first to love, while the other lagged behind a little. The latter may resent his partner for having in some measure persuaded him. As for the one who was the first to love, this fact caused him a kind of nervousness and uncertainty and he is never completely reassured. But on a deeper and more serious plane, what the other loves in me is rarely what I would want her to love. I would like to be loved in my essential difference, in what is most personal, most profound and most original in me. I want the other to show me myself and to be 'someone who is in me more myself than I am.' Hence the tendency of lovers always to confide to each other. There was a time when we did not know each other. We come from two different backgrounds. I want to tell all about my childhood, to show the house where I took my first steps, and I recall memories full of significance for me, but with very little meaning for others. In this way a dialogue tends to become a sequence of monologues where each is waiting with a secret impatience for the other to finish his story so that he can tell his own. Or else I find that she loves my hands which I have never noticed and which do not seem to me at all remarkable, while she is quite unmoved by my intelligence and my culture. To find that one's body is loved is usually a slightly bitter satisfaction, for we are more than a body, which is but the symbol of and means to a reality which goes beyond it. All lovers ask each other ' Who am I ? ' and the reply is most often disappointing because it is known to God alone.

But is not love itself, as I have conceived it from the start, an attack on God? Is it not sacrilegious for a man to demand from a woman, or a woman from a man what we can only and should only expect from God? We are ordered to turn away from creatures to the Creator. Here is a creature who suddenly captures our whole attention and we for our part hope to capture all of hers. It is here that Christian marriage intervenes for it is the sanctification of the urge of nature. But still it is important that a Christian marriage should not be based on a passionate choice only. For all passion is evil inasmuch as it takes our liberty from us. The dictates of wisdom agree here with the examples of sanctity. The wise man is master of himself and does not give in to his passions. As for the saint, he feels but one passion and that is directed towards God. He surrenders his liberty to him who has made him, and who furthermore gives it back as soon as it is surrendered to him, for there is no greater freedom than that of the children of God.

If the world is plunged into the most appalling confusion, it is only the result of the primeval confusion through which disobedient and sinful man chose to follow his own will in preference to the will of God. If Adam and Eve had been able to love each other outside the earthly paradise as they did within it, the sentence of banishment would have been lifted. The sword of King Mark, which separates Tristan and Isolde, is but the symbol of the flaming sword of the Seraphim who watch over the Garden of Eden. It is this which prevents the lover from being loved; this which makes even a misunderstanding the basis of a mutual love; this which surrounds perfect lovers with obstacles and which buried Romeo and Juliet in the tomb at Verona. If, however, these obstacles are overcome, then they are succeeded by those years which prove fatal to happy love. For we are unstable, subject to change, to growing old, and to death. See how she no longer speaks to me, and how I am no longer capable of experiencing my former emotions on seeing her. And I myself am changing. I see a critical eye looking me over; a mocking smile is flickering on those lips which formerly were so benevolent. But it needs less than this. It needs only the daily routine, habit, lack of effort. One no longer hopes for what one has; one no longer fears this homely and familiar being. Even jealousy eventually exhausts itself, or else it is no more than a selfish possessiveness towards what we consider to be our own property.

For these reasons I feel it would be a mistake to take this violent and exclusive attraction of one being with another as a basis for a Christian marriage. In the first place that would deprive marriage of its chief attribute : which is that it is contracted freely. The passionate lover cannot make a free choice. It is imposed on him as it were from outside. The answer which a betrothed Christian couple must give to him who solemnly questions them should be a free answer; there is no ' forgone conclusion ' that demands the marriage. That is why Claudel was quite right in making one of his characters say ' It is not love which makes a marriage, but consent.' ' Yes ' spoken in a moment of passion is not a free consent. A Christian marriage should be based on a kind of wisdom, and each of the parties should forget himself, not only for the sake of the other, but, even more, in the interests of a mystical shared task which they will work at together for the rest of their married life.

To what extent is the passionate recognition of one by the other a strong reason for marriage? It can just as easily be a mistake and a flash in the pan. I have tried to demonstrate some of the implications of such a recognition but it must be said that very frequently it is nothing but a passing fever of the heart and senses : something purely sentimental.

This comparison between love and an illness of the soul fills all the literature of love over the centuries. The conventional pictures of chains and captivity are well known. Beauty chains us to her sovereign throne. And if this illness and captivity are delightful, the dangers which they present are no less formidable. The soul takes pleasure in them and for nothing in the world would it be cured of its disease. Perhaps at bottom it is no more than a particularly poignant sign of sickness of life. The child has lived for a long time under the protection of its parents, warmly enclosed in the paternal house. There the years passed with extreme slowness; something still remained of the warmth of the mother's bosom.

And then, suddenly, the young boy or girl awakes to another destiny. The protective walls seem narrow and restraining. They try to climb over them and to look outside; they turn towards the vast unknown world, and find themselves alone. At this point appears the guiding soul which will ward off the long years of solitude to come. But how will this stranger react? How can it be arranged that this recognition of mine will also be a recognition for her? We are indeed no longer in the privileged state where the child never doubted the love of his parents, and indeed accepted it as his due. This creature is free and independent; she looks in every direction and there is nothing to indicate that she will condescend to let her eyes rest on me. I feel just how difficult life is in a world where nothing is acquired in advance, and where everything must be taken in a battle whose outcome is uncertain. Hence the frequently incalculable effects of a first unhappy love on a young man or woman.

And so metaphors of war succeed those which the language of love has borrowed from illness and captivity. To avoid being conquered it is necessary to conquer. The whole future depends on it. We give the name of happiness to this victory by which we rebuild the cell out of which we have just come, only with the woman of our choice, and far from the paternal home in which henceforth one is but a stranger. A failure here very easily results in despair, and it is not entirely inaccurate to speak of languishing and of dying of love. This does not only imply physical death or suicide. There are many ways of dying, and the worst is perhaps that which leads so many men and women to renounce love with bitterness, for from now on ' they know.'

They know what? What Peguy calls the great secret of men of forty: that man is not happy? But that is a knowledge which is more difficult to act on than it might seem. What they know, what they think they have learned in the course of an unhappy experience, is that one must not be made a fool of, and the person they consider to have been made a fool of is he or she who has given a great deal and who has received little in return A sordid and false view, for the one who gives most is indeed the one with most need, but also the one with the most interior riches. One should try to prevent one's heart from becoming mean. The reward of generosity is found not in the return of kindness but in our joy at the fact that we are able to give. One of the greatest pleasures in love is that it makes us want to give without counting the cost. It opens an inexhaustible spring in us. Whether these gifts are accepted or refused is really only of secondary importance. The essential thing is the gift itself. He is indeed unfortunate who refuses to give any more for fear of being imposed upon.

Certainly, it can and does happen that the recipient is overwhelmed by the abundance of these gifts : he did not ask for them; he had never expected so much. The more generous a love is, the more risk it runs of being rejected. It is said that gratitude is one of the virtues which men find most difficult to put into practice. Some proud spirits never want to be obliged to anyone for anything and feel humiliated whenever they find themselves in the position of not being able to give more than they have received, or at least as much. Perhaps it takes even more generosity to receive than to give. A happy love would be one between two equal generosities. It matters little that one gives more and the other less. Neither calculates; each is ready to give and to receive in a limitless exchange. Only small-minded people are overwhelmed by receiving, but they must be reckoned with, and we have less right to condemn them when we consider that in the face of God's gift we all show ourselves to be small-minded.

And so we find ourselves once more returned to this model for all love, the love of God for man. For one of the essential roles of human love is to disappoint us in order to turn us towards the one unique and real love. This lack of sufficiency must be accepted, and it is perhaps in its acceptance that the seriousness and sanctity of marriage is to be found. That is why I would like to see a sort of novitiate before marriage, as before undertaking religious vows. By this I do not mean a long engagement, which presents as many disadvantages as advantages. But marriage should be contracted without illusions and in a state of perfect serenity. The pessimists will say that in that case no one would ever marry. I think they are wrong. This permanent society of man and woman, in a Christian climate, is a society in which they are never alone. I do not allude here to the children who will come to people their solitude. I mean that between a Christian husband and wife, whether they have no descendants, or whether they are surrounded by many children, the presence of God continually creates this third dimension without which there is no perfect love.

For man is not the final end of woman, nor woman the final end of man, but God alone is the end of one and the other. If man seeks his final fulfilment in woman and vice versa, they will find only that desert which François Mauriac called to mind in the title of one of his novels. The creature in itself is sterile, instable, contradictory. The reasons which led us to love him can very easily be reversed and lead us to hate him. One moves from love to hate with disconcerting ease, or to indifference, which is worse still. It can happen that two lovers who have ceased to love each other promise mutual friendship. But this is a promise which is very rarely kept: one of those verbal formulae by which man hides from himself his greatest failures. Besides, it wrongs friendship to consider it as being a successor to love or something which is substituted when love is not possible. Language is constructed in such a way that one would think there was a hierarchy of sentiments in which friendship occupies a place immediately below that of love. One says of someone one does not love that one only feels friendship for him. I think on the contrary that the most desirable feeling between husband and wife is precisely this despised friendship.

For marriage is constructed to last, whereas love is built on the instant — one loves in a moment. Perhaps some time is necessary before one realises the fact. But some romantic image of a day long past is what has forever touched your heart, some detail which can easily be found by searching through one's memories. Moreover, in the happiest cases, love only procures moments of perfection. Between these moments stretch bitter solitudes, periods of doubt and of dissatisfaction. The graph of love is chaotic in the extreme, and we did not need Proust to tell us about what he calls ' the intermittences of the heart.' Marriage gives to all this stability and permanence. Certainly, whatever the intrinsic strength of the sacrament may be, it cannot change our psychology. Everyday life, habit, satiety attack Christian husbands and wives as any others. The fact is that what yesterday was a free gift, and delightful in the extent to which it was free, has today become a sort of duty which one has not the liberty to refuse; and this gives to the relationship of husband and wife an almost unique character; it was this duty that the Countess of Champagne, presiding over a Court of Love in 1174, judged, not without reason, to be incompatible with love as she saw it, and which she thought should remain an entirely free gift.

But the countess's point of view is sophisticated, and it would be easy to answer it, for one can plead just as well that nothing is free between lovers since they no longer have the possibility of refusing anything to each other without inflicting on themselves an appalling violence. Instead of this, husband and wife chose each other freely, and, in fact, the lack of this freedom is sufficient grounds for the granting of annulments by Church authorities. The characteristic of human freedom is to be able to renounce self. Committing oneself in marriage is not unlike following the evangelical counsels fully. While in the latter case men or women unite in chastity, obedience, and poverty to help each other either by pious exercises or by charitable works towards the love of God, in the former case a man and a woman exchange promises of mutual and perpetual fidelity with a view to propagating the human race, to call new souls into existence and to help each other to attain by way of the stages of human love the heights of the love of God.

In this way husband and wife do not take each other for an end, but they go beyond each other at the same time towards their progeny and towards charity. Christian marriage is thus founded on the renunciation of what is the end of profane love, a kind of sacrilegious adoration of the creature by the creature. Sanctified human love must transcend and sublimate itself. It is through not having clearly understood this that so many marriages fail. In no case can marriage be considered as the achievement and crowning of profane love, but rather as its transformation.

However, our potentialities for love are not necessarily exhausted at the moment marriage is celebrated. This meeting where two souls burn, or believe themselves to burn, with the same fire can happen after marriage, outside it. This is the theme which fills a considerable part of the literature of the world, and which is also found in real life. Adultery presupposes marriage, and there are many kinds of adultery. Even the simple casual affair, which only sets in motion the senses, and which is a betrayal of the body without necessarily being an infidelity of the soul, can lead to deeper and more real betrayals because the soul is always gravely affected by its own weakness. On consideration it is virtually impossible for one being always to satisfy another, and it is this which gives the pessimists a certain amount of reason when they say that if marriage were fully considered it would never be embarked upon.

Doubtless there is in every human being a dimension of infinity; every personality is inexhaustible, and in this sense it may be said that a husband never knows his wife, and vice versa. It is, then, possible to envisage a marriage in which husband and wife would never tire of each other because they will always have something to discover in one another. Why is it that such marriages are the exception rather than the rule? Because there is also in every human being a finite dimension. He is subject to change through time and also tends to fall too easily into habits and conventions. Familiarity breeds contempt. How many husbands and wives, after some years, literally no longer recognise each other! They are absorbed by a thousand preoccupations, which they no doubt share; but this sharing of preoccupations is not exactly what was envisaged at the beginning. In the extent to which we are movement and change, habit breeds boredom; this is another form, and a no less pernicious one, of sickness of life.

This illness was first experienced as a kind of anxiety, when for the first time we met this unknown person on whose answer all our fate depended. Now it has developed into weariness. There is no longer anything to be discovered in a being who has already given us everything. One tries to escape, and the escaping of the forty-year-old is infinitely more dangerous than that of the adolescent. This is the famous ' demon of middle age ', swollen with as many regrets as the other was with hopes. Is there not still time to succeed in life? Must we lose this last chance offered to us, and set off with no looking back, along the road which brings us more and more quickly to old age and death? There is almost always a last chance on the threshold of old age, as there was a first chance

at the entrance to adult life. We know the tragic
frenzy of this autumn love for someone who is
younger and who (we do not even attempt to deceive
ourselves about it) will sooner or later be unfaithful.

To love, does it not mean to live and live fully?
Just at the moment that life seems to be passing us
by, we are tempted to hold on to it through love, but
in most cases a love which is outside marriage. For
our wife has grown old with us, and it is not she who
can cause the fountain of youth to flow. If marriage
then seems like a prison, a chain too heavy to bear,
and whose links are wearing into the flesh, it is
because we have built it on a false idea of happiness
and of love, which gave too important a place to
desire. Happiness is not to satisfy one's desire, for
there is nothing more boring than a desire fulfilled,
and Claudel was quite right in saying in this sense,
that there is nothing of which man tires so quickly
as happiness. We should not, then, be surprised to see
apparently cloudless marriages break up : the reasons
to be found in their false idea of happiness.

Simone Weil has rightly said that only the universal
deserves our love, but that we are able to love only
the particular. The mistake of human love is to
attempt continually to transfer to the particular what
is the prerogative of the uinversal. It is natural that,
in these circumstances, the particular should deceive
us and that we should chase in vain that which God
alone is in a position to give us. This is the tragedy
of Don Juan. Marriage is the solution to this problem,
provided that husband and wife do not regard each

other as an end in themselves, but that each agrees to transcend the limits of the other, and to be transcended by him. Then indeed each will find in the other a constant newness; and even our weaknesses, far from separating us, will attach us still more closely.

In other words the earthly object of our love must never become for us an idol. But man has such a power for adoration that he must always take care lest it turn from its invisible object to attach itself to a visible object. The idol is at once tyrannical and tyrannised. One demands of it what it cannot give, until the day comes when one smashes it in rage and overwhelms it with abuse simply because one had given it too much. One element of love has quite been forgotten, one which Simone Weil has again rightly stressed : compassion. Compassion is essential, and, on reflection, it is obvious that there is no love in which it does not play a large part. It is compassion which is at the bottom of tenderness, and tenderness itself is the purification of desire.

This being which today is so beautiful in our eyes would not move us to such an extent if we did not know it to be mortal and perishable. It is this fragility, and this insubstantiality which makes it infinitely precious to us; and what turns us away from the love of God is not only that he is invisible, but still more that he is eternal and unchanging and we cannot quite believe that he really does need us. Only the Incarnation and the contemplation of a dying and crucified God allow us to feel for him this tenderness without which there can be no real love. But, in the human being of our choice, everything calls forth compassion and tenderness. The most sincere expressions of love bear this characteristic. There is a deep sadness in the fact of being a man or a woman, destined to suffering, to ageing and to death. There is in the other person a loneliness which we cannot penetrate, an essential retreat, the door of which is forbidden to us, and where he suffers far from us, without our being able to do anything but contemplate this mute and intangible sorrow.

It is not only the need which I formerly had of her which made me love this woman, but also the need which she felt for me. A need which neither one nor the other can satisfy, and which is the principle of a perpetual renewal. In this sense it may be said that husband and wife only take each other in marriage on the cross. A truth which does not sound hard to him who knows how to listen to it, for it expresses simply a fundamental aspect of Christian marriage: to know that husband should love his wife as Christ loves the Church, and wife should love her husband as the Church loves Christ. But to admit this it is necessary to change radically the current idea of love. Love is not just admiration and desire, but a still more essential need to serve and to fulfil oneself by losing oneself. The one I love above all others is the one who has the greatest need of me, and who believes that she could not live without me. Doubtless she is wrong and I am not as necessary to her as she thinks. But it is not for me to judge, and it is right that need should evoke the love that is born of compassion. Similarly I too need to be needed; without this I should be of no use in this world. This need engenders compassion, and compassion engenders need in a sort of endless chain.

The perfection of man here on earth is without doubt to find and fulfil his vocation. The young man and the young woman are seeking it, with restlessly beating hearts. Marriage gives it to them, and there is truly no better part for them than that which they have chosen. At each instant of their common life, however long it may last, they should remake in their hearts the choice which was made once, for it is inexhaustible since the sacrament is perpetual. The scars of illness and age change nothing; on the contrary, they render even more compelling the need which first drew us. We will discover that this need was infinite, and that we are infinitely powerless to satisfy it, since there is always something which we cannot supply. But if we bring all our good will to bear on it God will supply the rest.

In this matter nature deceives us and God himself places around us snares which draw us where we do not want to go. It is not enough to say that man only fulfils himself in surpassing himself; he only fulfils himself by renouncing himself. Marriage is a means of renunciation like the religious life. All the characteristics of love can be reviewed in this perspective. There was the desire to conquer, to possess and to assert oneself; but if it remains thus man is doomed to disappointment and death. On the contrary, to conquer is to be conquered, not by a greater strength, but by a weakness such that we cannot resist it; to possess is to be possessed, invested with the need the other has of oneself; to assert oneself is simply to put oneself in the place where one is required to serve. The daily round is then transfigured and the path is no longer boring, even though it still has obstacles. Fundamentally the whole problem of man is to go beyond his own horizons.

For all that, love is the best or the worst of things and its mystery lies in this very fact. What is important is not to know at the moment of its birth whether it will be happy or unhappy, for as much benefit can be drawn from an unhappy love as from a happy one. But whether or not it will succeed in surpassing itself and blossoming out into charity, or whether it will turn back to its own object, seeking to exhaust the inexhaustible and to constrain liberty, love like everything human contains opposing assumptions, and it is with good reason that it has so often been represented as the brother of death. It aims to control the loved one; it aims also to exalt her. It has also been found to be very close to hatred, and indeed in every highly-charged love there are dark passages of hatred. Only indifference is forbidden, for indifference is death and fixity, whereas love is the embodiment of movement and change.

Love also involves attachment, exclusive attachment, and in this it is the antithesis of that detachment which is the goal of all Christian asceticism. But it comprises also an aspect of detachment since it detaches us from everything which is not its object. ' One person is missing and for us the whole world is empty.' In this it can cause us to understand the vanity of all human desires. The true lover is in the position of a mystic who loves only God and for whom all creatures are savourless; except that he has chosen among all the others a privileged creature who takes the place of all the others and even tries to usurp God's position. If she succeeds we witness the installing of hell within us, for hell here on earth is nothing other than having God hidden from us by his creatures.

One other way out is fortunately possible. The land of hunger and thirst (that is, the desire which creatures awaken in us) contains rocks whence the holy staff can cause thirst-quenching waters to gush, and it is not impossible that we may be fed by heavenly manna. This will happen on condition that we do not take this desert to be our true fatherland and that we aspire to the Promised Land, to which this desert is but a road, and it is to this that Christian marriage invites them, calling God to witness the most human attachments. Now love is transfigured and all which was obscure becomes full of light. The beauty of this woman who formerly charmed me is no more than the reflection of beauty incarnate. All becomes sign and symbol, and our bodies themselves are no more than the perishable instruments of a process which goes beyond them and explains their rightful condemnation to old age and death. Maternity confirms the wife's dignity, just as paternity confirms her husband's. Sensuality is vanquished in the very moment of its apparent triumph; the *Fiat* of the Virgin Mary is not out of place on the lips of husband and wife on the day on which they offer a newborn life to God.

Love between them has now become friendship, not by a degradation, but on the contrary by a transfiguration. If love involves conflict, friendship does not. Here there is no hatred of the other, no desire to suppress or absorb him, but simply to do him good. In certain languages to say that one loves a person one says one wishes him well. An admirable expression, but one which is far more true of friendship than of love on its first spring. To wish well to someone is to forget oneself in order to put oneself in his place and prefer what is good for him to what is good for oneself. Attachment thus becomes detachment; covetousness has become charity; desire has become need, not of taking but of giving; violence is changed into tenderness. It is no longer in the glance of the other that henceforth I seek my happiness, but in the fact that our two glances meet at the horizon of earthly life, stretched towards the same goal, in a desire which earth cannot destroy.

It is not good for man to be alone. That is why men unite and form between them every kind of society, whose final end should be to help each other towards the possession of the only real good. Marriage is the most natural and the oldest of these societies. Although it must be based on mutual love, one must nevertheless remember that in our state as fallen

creatures, always menaced by the triple concupiscence, human love ought to be transcended, and not
become its own end. This is an asceticism which is
sometimes difficult, but which life imposes. Those
who try to escape it not only endanger their health,
but also this lowly portion of earthly happiness which
is not refused to us on condition that we learn to
welcome it with a humble and contrite heart, the
heart which God does not despise. We must finally
understand that, following the memorable saying of
Lacordaire, ' there is only one love ', and that this
lightning which flashed between two creatures is the
symbol of another light. The family perpetuates this
brightness and warmth until the day when the veils
of flesh will part, and when the fugitive instant
becomes eternity.